HOW TO MAKE A KILLING
IN NEW ISSUES

HOW TO MAKE A KILLING IN NEW ISSUES

MICHAEL WALTERS

SIDGWICK & JACKSON

LONDON

To Mike, who tells me he taught me all I know

First published in Great Britain in 1988 by
Sidgwick & Jackson Limited
1 Tavistock Chambers, Bloomsbury Way
London WC1A 2SG

ISBN 0 283 99620 X

Phototypeset by Rowland Phototypesetting Limited
Bury St Edmunds, Suffolk

Printed in Great Britain by Adlard & Son Limited
The Garden City Press, Letchworth, Herts.
for Sidgwick & Jackson Limited
1 Tavistock Chambers, Bloomsbury Way
London WC1A 2SG

Contents

Introduction

New issues? A killing in new issues? After the Great Crash of '87, when the London market lost 25 per cent of its value in a couple of weeks? And when the £7.2bn State sell-off of British Petroleum laid a colossal egg, forcing the Chancellor to arrange for the Bank of England to bail out unwise applicants by buying at 70p the new shares that they had picked up at 120p? What a joke!

Or is it? The one sure thing in the stock market is that *nothing* stays the same. The picture is always changing. Everyone took a dreadful battering in the autumn of 1987 on issues both old and new. Hopefully, everyone who ventures into the share jungle is now a little wiser, a little more cautious – and a whole lot better-equipped to cope with the dangers.

What *is* certain is that the good times will come again, sooner or later. They may be back by the time you are reading this – and you will need to be ready to take advantage of them. The new issue game is a wonderful way of making money, with limited risk – when it is right. And one thing is certain in the wake of the Great Crash of '87. New issues are going to be a cheaper, better value than they ever were in the first nine months of 1987.

Can you imagine the nail-biting among those charged with putting together the privatization issues which follow the BP flop? As the government and the issuing houses grew greedier as 1987 progressed, who will dare risk pricing an issue too finely in the years to follow? The political must decree that to push ahead with wider share ownership, post-BP, the State sell-offs will be back to bargain terms.

One can imagine that similar considerations will be influencing any private company coming to market. Make it cheaper, keep it cheerful. So the great new issue game is far from over. There will be killings galore to be made in new issues, at the right time. The lesson of autumn '87 was a hard one, but more people than ever are alive – not just to the pitfalls, but also, to the profit potential.

Cast your mind back to the days before the Crash. The headlines said it all – 'British Airways Shares Take Off', 'Instant Profit on British Gas', and 'Millions Chase Sock Shop Shares'. New issue news was the topic that half the nation was talking about – the chance of a killing in the new issue market.

Win or lose, the private investor *has* been bounding back into the stock market in recent years. Wherever you go, there is someone with shares in British Telecom, who went for the Jaguar flotation, who won with British Airways, or who shopped at Tie Rack, loved Laura Ashley, and had to have a go when the shares came up for sale.

Nearly 10 million people owned shares by the autumn of 1987. A vast number of them started by buying new issues. They really began to catch on towards the end of 1984 with British Telecom, the first great privatization. Playing the new issue game quickly became a super way of supplementing the income, making a little extra for the holidays. The big market players who have always known about new issues have made millions of pounds in profits – quite literally – year after year. Suddenly the small investor was in there with a vengeance, jostling alongside the big boys to snatch at the pennies.

Telecom really opened it up for the small investor. Who could beat it? Two million investors picked up a piece of Telecom in the autumn of 1984. For every 100p they put in, they had a profit of 86p on the first day of dealing. If they held on, a few months later there was a profit of 140p for every 100p. Magic, pure magic. Pound notes for 50p – or less.

Since then, almost everyone has become street-smart – Throgmorton Street-smart – about new issues. The chance of making £30, £40, or even £100 for simply filling in a form and getting it in on time lured in all sorts of players, young and old. BP was bad news. But it took no great genius to spot that it was in trouble before it began. Almost every newspaper sounded the warning. Reading the press and using a little common sense helped keep most people out of trouble.

The State sell-offs, of course, have led the way in opening up the market. So they should, given the fortune the Government has spent on launching them. Sid was everywhere and nowhere in the autumn of 1986 as a hard-sell campaign hit the press and television screens. 'If you see Sid, tell him . . .' became a national catch-phrase. It irritated and upset hundreds of thousands of people, but got them talking, made them aware that the government was selling British Gas shares. Love Sid or loathe him, millions knew he meant there was a bargain to be had in Gas. And the applications poured in. If you got the 50p paid shares, you were able to sell them as soon as dealings started for around 67p. That soothed the pain of putting up with Sid.

The selling power behind privatization means all but BP have been massively over-subscribed, even when the government has pretended not to want to push them too hard to the small investor. The relatively risky nature of the business of British Airways prompted some pretence that this was not aimed at the small man. So they cut down the advertising spend. It did not stop commercials filling our television screens for weeks ahead of the issue, nor prevent them from flying Concorde low over Buckingham Palace while they released masses of balloons at a giant press conference below. Nor did it discourage Saatchi & Saatchi from grabbing prime television news time by erecting a great globe on the River Thames and lighting up the London skies with fireworks and a laser show.

Millions rushed for the shares, and clinched a fat profit for their trouble, many blissfully unaware that British Airways is a business whose profits could plunge at any moment, if any of a whole string of problems suddenly surfaced. Most did not give it a thought. Why should they? They knew the game. It was privatization time. The government was giving money away once more. It made sense to grab some. You could hardly go wrong, could you?

It was not quite so easy with British Airports Authority. Not only was there a tricky, untried tender system for part of the issue, but they also sprang an unexpectedly low cut-off point on unsuspecting stags. Out of the blue, anyone meaning to invest more than £1,000 was knocked out, given no shares at all. Hundreds of thousands of applications went unrewarded, and cheques were returned uncashed, with no quick killing. Others who misread the tender, or simply misunderstood it and bid too much for the shares, found that within weeks the price had fallen below what they had paid. Suddenly there was a State privatization issue showing a loss for the unwary.

Even for those who succeeded in getting shares, the game was scarcely worth the candle. Most applicants were given only 100 shares, so even an opening price of 140p for shares which cost 100p left precious little profit, after dealing expenses. It was a risk-free return, if you got it right, and still worth having. But if you pitched your British Airports application wrongly, you had a problem – one that perhaps this book could have helped you escape.

Most of the privatizations, though, have been big winners. The list below (which includes the pseudo-privatization of the Trustee Savings Bank) shows that the tricky State sell-offs have often been the oil companies. Almost all of the others have been very nearly as good as cash in the hand.

COMPANY	DATE	PRICE	OPENING PRICE	PRICE OCT 1st 1987
British Aerospace	Feb. 1981	Fixed 150p	175p	540p
British Aerospace	May 1985	Fixed 375p		540p
		Part-paid 200p	244p	
Cable & Wireless	Nov. 1981	Fixed 56p*	64½p	495p
Cable & Wireless	Dec. 1983	Tender 137½p*		
		Part-paid 100p*	98p	
Cable & Wireless	Dec. 1985	Fixed 293p*	153p	495p
		Part-paid 150p*		
Amersham International	Feb. 1982	Fixed 142p	192p	637p
Britoil	Nov. 1982	Tender 215p	196p	331p
		Part-paid 100p	81p	
Britoil	Aug. 1985	Fixed 185p	207p	331p
		Part-paid 100p	122p	
Associated British Ports	Feb. 1983	Fixed 56p*	68p	637p
Associated British Ports	Apr. 1984	Tender	135p	637p
		Part-paid 100p*	102p	
Enterprise Oil	Jul. 1984	Tender 185p	186p	335p
Jaguar	Aug. 1984	Fixed 165p	177p	572p
British Telecom	Dec. 1984	Fixed 130p	168p	273p
		Part-paid 50p	93p	
Trustee Savings		Fixed 100p	135p	139p
British Gas	Dec. 1986	Fixed 135p	152p	174p
		Part-paid 50p	67p	
British Airways	Feb. 1987	Fixed 125p	169p	217p
		Part-paid 65p	109p	
Rolls-Royce	May 1987	Fixed 170p	232p	210p
British Airports	Jul. 1987	Part-paid 100p	140p	143p
		Tender part-paid at least 142p	140p	143p

Adjusted for capital changes.

It is not just the privatizations, the State sell-offs, where there is easy money to be made. Only Virgin, Richard Branson's records to shops group, has so far made any real attempt at the big television share sell – and that got a little sticky when they used the complicated tender system to set the price. But a whole host of other companies have been going public, and offering straightforward rich rewards for those who picked the right ones.

To take just a few, with winners like banana importers Geest there was an instant gain of 28p on the 125p issue price. Or pharmaceuticals giant Wellcome, with a first-day dealing profit of 52p on the 120p issue price. Those are the bigger names, offers for sale on the main market. Beneath them, there are companies which sailed happily on to the Unlisted Securities Market, like TV-am, with an opening premium of 11p. There are dozens of smaller companies floated more quietly, by a placing. It may be almost impossible to get them at the issue price. But the shrewd investor can make a killing by picking them up in the market on the first day of dealing.

Obviously shares in the High Street names everyone knows have been easiest to sell, and have attracted the greatest mass of money. Laura Ashley was one of the biggest winners, coming to market in 1985 with a flair which has since been largely absent from the company's stock market career. But when Laura Ashley launched, it launched big. Anyone who bought shares for 135p in the flotation was able to sell at 185p on the first day of dealing. Wonderful.

The High Street follow-through came in the spring and summer of 1987, when the stock market was ablaze and ripe for two amazing little flotations. Sock Shop and Tie Rack both carved an astonishing growth pattern, mainly across the London retail scene. Their bright little shops selling socks and ties, but little else, caught everyone's eye. When Sock Shop offered a tiny 3.9 million shares for sale at 125p each, it pulled in applications for 206 million. The issue attracted a massive £260 million. When dealings started, the shares doubled on the first day. Anyone lucky enough to get any made an instant killing.

Tie Rack was trickier, and illustrates that it is not always enough just to follow the crowd. A little care and extra consideration – seeking the kind of clues a book like this can help you find – can pay off. Rather larger and longer-established than Sock Shop – the Sock Shop proprietors once worked at Tie Rack – the company was still fairly small and new. It floated 8.6 million shares at 145p each. Again, the rush was hectic, and the issue attracted £1 billion, with applications for 728 million shares. When dealings started, however, there was a touch of disappointment. Issued at 145p, the shares touched 201p, and began to fall away. A couple of months later, they were hovering below the issue price. There was a killing for the swift, but a more modest killing than many had expected.

What went wrong? The Tie Rack team overcooked it. They bungled the issue press conference, and some journalists quickly fastened on to the fine print. Tucked away there sat a mystery group of Swiss investors with 49 per cent of the company – effective control. Chairman Roy Bishko insisted they would not interfere, but no one established quite who they were. Their presence raised question marks. Tie Rack, too, left unanswered questions about the pace of short-term profits growth. That, plus the remarkably high rating demanded for the shares, took the shine off for the professionals.

The result? A new issue which looked a sure-fire winner turned lame. Instead of a massive profit for all, there was a loss for the laggard who failed to sell before it turned a little sour.

Never mind. When the stock market is in reasonable mood, the vast proportion of new issues show instant profits for those who manage to get hold of them. But the game can be played all the better with a degree of skill. Anyone who thinks carefully about the new issue game and watches what is going on can swing an already favourable set of odds still further their way. There can be no guarantee that you will be able to dodge every loser, but it does not take too much specialist knowledge to spot the trickier issues and to steer clear of them. And even when new issues do turn sour, the initial losses are rarely substantial. Once again, look at BP. A massive flop – but even then the Chancellor stepped in to limit everyone's losses.

This book offers no guarantees. But it contains practical advice on the pluses and minuses of the new issue game. There are times when making money in new issues seems as easy as falling off a log. Perhaps it is. Sometimes – just sometimes – you might break your neck when you fall. Perhaps this book can help you make a more comfortable landing. Good luck.

1 Are New Issues For You?

New issues floated on the London Stock Exchange are the ideal way into direct share ownership. Easy to buy, relatively low-risk, and almost always under-priced. What could be better?

All you need to do is clip the coupon out of your national newspaper, or telephone a share information office and they will send you a prospectus with full details of the company, and an application form to post off. You hardly need to know what the company does, scarcely need bother to read the fact-packed pages in the prospectus or the great slugs of fine print in the newspaper. You really only need to know whether the City thinks this is a good thing, and you can clamber on board. These days, if you read your favourite City page, news of any sizeable share flotation will come complete with advice on whether or not it looks like succeeding. The financial press does not get it right every time, but does pretty well. All you need to do is to follow the herd. If the herd is going for it, then sheer weight of numbers, sheer money power, will ensure that the issue goes well.

There is none of the fuss and bother of finding a stockbroker to buy for you, or going to your bank to arrange a deal. And there are none of the costs that come with buying shares which are already listed, when you pay commission to a broker (£15 or £20 minimum), VAT, and stamp duty. In the case of a new issue, simply fill in a form, write out a cheque, and pop it in the post. All being well, a few days later you will read how much money has been chasing the shares, and how many you are likely to get. A few days more, and an allotment letter comes through the post, telling you how many shares you have got. If you were unlucky, and did not get any, or not as many as you wanted, back comes a cheque for whatever you are owed. Dealings should have started on the stock market on the day you get your allotment letter. Check the City page for the price, and you can see how much money you have made for your trouble.

It is socially responsible, and politically acceptable too, to put money into a new issue of shares, because you will often be helping to

1

expand the business, providing more jobs, and generally backing British industry. Under the Tory government, the idea is to encourage the growth of a share-owning democracy in a process that will unite the interests of workers, employers and the providers of capital. New shareholders should ideally take an interest in the companies whose shares they buy, cheer them on from the side-lines – and if they vote Tory too, so much the better. The privatization issues have generally been heavily slanted towards recruiting the new, smaller investor. Bonus schemes offering one free share for every ten to those holding on to the privatization issues for three years, have made it clear that the government wants to see the new shareholders in the market to stay.

THE DANGERS

All well and good. But are new issues for you? Since shares can and do fall as well as rise in value, should you be putting your savings into them? Relatively few public companies go bust, leaving shareholders with nothing. In the 1980s, perhaps half a dozen a year have failed, on average. In the late 1980s, the figures have been even more comforting. Hardly a quoted company has gone to the wall in 1986 and 1987. And while there have been one or two casualties among newcomers to the Unlisted Securities Market in the 1980s, no new issue floated on the Stock Exchange main market has come a complete cropper for many years.

That is not to say that there are no risks involved in the new issue game. There are. Investing in any share is risky. The autumn of 1987 brought a nasty reminder to many of the investors who had been sucked into the market in the eighties – many of them buying shares first through one of the great privatization issues like British Telecom.

Suddenly, in one dramatic week in the middle of October, investors who had become accustomed to share prices rising – suffering perhaps the occasional hiccup, and then recovering their poise – were hit by a hurricane – quite literally for those who lived in the South of England. One Friday morning, they woke to find roofs smashed, trees uprooted everywhere, electricity lines down, telephones out and rail services halted. Many City folk failed to make it to work, and the Bank of England hurriedly declared an emergency bank holiday.

The stock market mood had been uneasy. Poor trade figures in mid-week had unsettled the American market. And then the Japanese began selling in America. Wall Street moved sharply down. In London, those who struggled in after spending the weekend clearing up the hurricane damage around their homes found shares in free fall.

The *Financial Times* Stock Exchange 100 Share Index lost 250 points on the Monday, and again on the Tuesday. Previously, it had never moved more than 70 points in one session.

It was all too much for a market that had risen by nearly 50 per cent since the beginning of the year, and where old hands had long been muttering about the frothy, insubstantial basis for some rises. In one week, share values lost £100,000 million. The newer, less experienced investors were among those hardest hit. Encouraged by easy profits, many had rapidly begun to increase the size of their deals. And people who had begun playing with £1,000 a time had made money and gone on to dabble in £5,000 lots, then £10,000, and maybe more, often hoping to sell before they had to pay for the shares they had bought. All at once, they found prices had turned sharply against them, and, most frightening of all, it was well-nigh impossible to sell many of their more speculative shares. They were trapped, needing to sell to pay their brokers, but suddenly no-one would buy.

Panic struck. Many lost tens of thousands of pounds. A few lost millions. Everywhere there were tales of market professionals, younger brokers and fund managers, being forced to sell fancy cars and mortgage houses to meet broking bills running to £100,000 or more.

In a few grim days, they were forced to learn the hard way that talk about share investment being a risky business really does count, really does mean what it says. In the riskier reaches of the traded option market, a 23 year-old trainee accountant went down for £1 million. One stockbroker lost £4 million for himself and his clients. Even a 15 year-old schoolboy hit the headlines with losses of £20,000 playing shares.

Even if you simply want to play the new issue game, buying shares as they are launched, and selling straight away, the message holds good – trading in shares is a risky business. You should only do it with money you can afford to lose. Provided you stick to shares which are traded on the London Stock Exchange – a vital, never-to-be-ignored qualification – the risks in new issues are much lower than in the average share. If you are intending to stag an issue – the market slang for applying for shares and selling out as soon as dealings start – you can afford to use borrowed money, to a carefully limited extent. That technique is something I discuss in detail later. But never forget that you are taking a risk, with any shares at any time.

CAN YOU AFFORD IT?

So make sure that you can afford to pay before you begin to play. That means getting down to the basics of your financial position. First you must ensure that you have ample income to cover the outgoings on the roof over your head – the mortgage or the rent. If you have a mortgage, you will almost certainly have a mortgage protection policy, which pays off the outstanding amount of your loan on your death. Make sure. That is essential to anyone with a family.

Life assurance comes next, for both husband and wife in any family. The experts recommend that the main wage-earner insures his or her life for around ten times annual salary. That may make the premiums a bit steep for some. But think about it. There is less publicity, and less selling pressure urging people to take out permanent health insurance. But it is important to try to ensure that there is some source of continuing guaranteed cash coming into the house should the main breadwinner fall ill, or become incapacitated. The cost of such policies can be reduced sharply by agreeing that the income be deferred for six months or a year after the problem first arises. Do take one out.

Naturally, proper attention should be paid to pension arrangements. These are coming in for a wave of publicity now with the government's new Personal Pension plans. It sounds boring, but go to an independent adviser, and make sure you get it right.

What then? Obviously everyone should have that extra something tucked away for a rainy day. Make sure it is somewhere absolutely safe and sound. Not under the bed, but in a building society account, or one of the big High Street banks. Think about it, though. They pay interest after deducting tax. If you pay tax at less than standard rate, you are losing out. The best return of all, with absolute safety, comes from the National Savings Bank. They pay interest before taking off tax – an especially useful deal for pensioners and others on low incomes.

Above all, do not be tempted by advertisements offering higher rates of interest than those advertised by the well-known banks and building societies. The one immutable law of the investment world is 'The higher the return, the greater the risk'. Do not seek to do anything ambitious with your basic savings. Just make sure they are safe, and somewhere handy where you can get at them quickly and easily when you need them.

PERSONAL EQUITY PLANS

Next in line for any prudent investor's personal financial survival kit should come either one of the government's relatively new ideas – the Personal Equity Plan – or a stake in a good, solid middle-of-the-road unit trust.

In my book *How To Profit From Your Personal Equity Plan* (Sidgwick & Jackson, £5.95), I explain in detail how to set about choosing the most suitable PEP. Put simply, the PEP allows anyone over the age of 18 to invest up to £2,400 in shares, and to take the income and capital growth from them free of any tax, provided that the PEP is operated for at least one full calendar year. You can either pick the shares yourself, or go to one of the many experienced investment firms who will operate the plan for you.

I recommend that you pick a PEP with a management company that has a good, solid, long-term record. My favourites of the schemes on offer in the Autumn of 1987 (new schemes are being issued regularly) are run by unit trust group Save & Prosper, the Prudential, and, for those prepared to pay higher charges for more detailed comment and guidance, Fidelity. All of the big banks have their managed PEPs, and Barclays has made a special effort to please.

All of the managed PEPs pick a limited number of top shares – usually between four and twenty – and buy them on your behalf. Pick a reputable group, and you should have no worry. Once again, though, because the PEPs are investing in shares, their value may fall as well as rise. Over the long term, though, they should generate a combination of capital growth and income that should substantially outpace the returns from a bank or building society deposit account.

UNIT TRUSTS

Similar observations apply to unit trusts, which invest in a wide range of shares on behalf of their unit-holders, creating units whose value rises or falls in line with the value of the shares the trust has bought. They have a wider spread of investment than PEPs, and so should offer greater security. Unfortunately, there are now more than 1,000 of them, many specializing in somewhat esoteric and risky sectors of the world stock markets. These can produce scorching capital growth – and sharp capital losses. Keep clear of the exotics. Stick to a standard, middle-of-the-road British or international trust aiming at solid capital growth. Before you buy, examine the past record of the managers and of the fund. Past performance is no guarantee of future competence, but it is the best guide you are going to get.

My personal choice would be the general funds from giants like Save & Prosper, M & G, the Prudential, GT Management, or the enterprising Perpetual. Once again, there are no guarantees. The best manager in the world will not make money for unit-holders when stock markets around the world are miserable. But unit trusts are a worthwhile way of protecting a chunk of your capital from inflation, and of earning real growth over the medium to long term. They also take the worry out of do-it-yourself investment for beginners, and offer an invaluable window on to the way the share world works.

If I suggest buying a PEP before a unit trust, it is simply because the best PEPs have most of the advantages of unit trusts, plus the bonus of tax-free income and capital growth. That may not make much difference in the short to medium run, but over the years it could be a plus worth having.

INVESTMENT TRUSTS

The more sophisticated saver should look at investment trusts. Similar to unit trusts, these buy shares with the aim of making money out of them. The prices of investment trusts, however, are not governed by the value of the shares they hold. They have a fixed capital, and a limited number of shares in issue. The price of those shares – the investment trust shares – rises and falls according to demand. That, in turn, is influenced by how well the shares the investment trust owns are doing.

Usually, shares in the investment trust sell at a discount to asset value – that is, you can buy them for less than the value of the shares the trust holds. In recent years, many predators have bid for investment trusts to exploit this quirk, selling off the shares the trust holds, and taking the cash. The discount means that when you buy a share in an investment trust, you could be buying 120p of assets for every 100p you pay. In a unit trust, you pay 100p for 100p of assets. So that means investment trusts can be better value.

Investment trusts, then, are a more sophisticated form of unit trust. They repay a little study. The Association of Investment Trusts is extremely anxious that they should be more widely understood, and sends out a wealth of useful information. Write and ask for it at The Association of Investment Trust Companies, Park House, 6th floor, 16 Finsbury Circus, London EC2M 7JJ (telephone: 01-588 5347).

THE WAY YOU FEEL

Once you have sorted out your financial safety net, you need to decide how much you can afford to gamble with, and just how you feel about it. You can use as much or as little as you like. The massive autumn 1987 BP sale was pitched to encourage investments as low as £96. British Airports Authority doled out shares in £100 lots. There is no minimum, though under £250 hardly seems worth the trouble for any but the absolute beginners.

I use the word 'gamble' quite deliberately. Though buying shares in new issues, and especially privatizations, has acquired a new air of political and economic respectability, it still involves gambling. Do not fool yourself. You are betting that you can pick shares that will go up, rather than down, and sell them at a profit. You are taking a gamble. If that does not suit you, forget it. The whole business of investment comes preciously close to being a highly sophisticated form of gambling. BP brought that home with a bang.

Becoming a shareholder does change your perspective over a time. The Tory government certainly knows it. Shareholders are less likely to go on strike and risk disrupting the profits of the company they work for than non-shareholders. The business of buying shares certainly locks people in more firmly to the capitalist, private enterprise system, and shifts them ever so slightly to the right in political terms.

More important, however, for the prospective shareholder is the need to emphasize the risks once again, be they extremely small in new issues. It is possible to get it wrong. It is just possible to lose quite a lot of money if you play the new issue game stupidly. Never use money you cannot afford to lose.

I have lost money playing the share market. Believe me, it hurts. There are no excuses that matter, nothing you can do about it. In the end, you are forced to accept that you got it wrong. If you are not prepared to accept that possibility, do not play. No matter how careful you are, you will lose money on some deals. You can never cover all of the angles, never know enough. There is always the danger of getting hit by something completely unexpected, right out of the blue.

The Stock Exchange lives and dies by trading information. Shares rise as more people buy than sell. They fall when the supply of shares being sold exceeds the demand for them. That may sound a trite, elementary observation, but never forget it. For every buyer, there has to be a seller. What you are effectively doing when you buy a share, is betting that the seller has got it wrong. He may be selling for a whole variety of reasons, reasons that you may never be able to guess, and which may have nothing at all to do with any real notion of the value of the shares. But you will not know that. On the other hand, he may know that something is badly wrong with the company in question. He may know that before anyone else, and if you knew as much as he did, you would not be buying.

So never get too sure of yourself. The most careful, rational share purchase in the world may look completely crazy in the light of what emerges a week or two later. Be sure of only one thing – there is always someone who knows more than you do. Just so long as most people see things as you do, and there are more buyers than sellers, the price will be fine. The moment that balance changes, no matter how right you may think you are, the shares will fall – even if the sellers have got it wrong, and think they know something when they do not. It is no good being right about the business if you are wrong about the share price. In the end, the share price is all that determines whether you make money or lose it.

INSIDER TRADING

In practice, the dangers may not be even remotely so great, the situations never so fraught as I have suggested. Insider trading – the illegal use of privileged information to buy or sell shares – does exist. It will continue, no matter what the law says. But for most people, most of the time, the stock market operates reasonably fairly. In new issues, the dangers are even more modest. Stock Exchange rules determine very strictly what can be said when a company comes to market, and there are all manner of checks and cross-checks to ensure that investors know the true position. Nonetheless, the share price of some new issues goes rocketing, while others just splutter and slide lower. In the investment game, there are no absolutes, no guarantees. You can never be completely sure.

2   Why New Issues Offer Winning Value

Once you are sure you can take all of the uncertainties of the stock market in your stride, and have spare cash enough to cope, there are compelling reasons for dipping a toe into the new issue market. New issues are simply better value than the average share, whether you are going for the quick killing as a stag, or plan to take them up and stay some distance with them.

Stagging and the instant profits it brings may grab everyone's attention, but many investors buy new issues to have and to hold. In investment terms, building a portfolio through new issues alone makes a lot of sense. They are generally under-priced – quite deliberately. There are ifs and buts galore, but in normal circumstances the ideal issue is sold at about 10 per cent under what might otherwise be considered the proper price. The most successful issue from the seller's point of view is the one that arouses a good deal of interest, is subscribed, say, three times, and opens trading at 10 per cent or so above the issue price. Anything different, and the issue was either too cheap, or too dear.

This apparently uncharacteristic gesture of City generosity is, of course, nothing of the sort. It simply reflects the price you have to pay to be sure of getting a new issue away happily, and the issuing house knows it full well. An issue that is undersubscribed does not attract sufficient applications, and is forced to leave shares with underwriters. The underwriters are City professionals who agree to buy any spare shares in return for a small commission. By and large, they hate to pay, hate to be called upon to do their duty and pick up shares no one wants.

That is bad news for everyone. It means that the opening price may be at a discount, below the offer price, and everyone is left with a nasty taste. The vendors will still have gotten their money, thanks to the underwriters, but usually they will have kept a large chunk of the shares. They will be unhappy to see them valued at less than they had been led to expect. Anyone who applied to buy shares will be facing an instant loss. The issuing house will be looking foolish, hard-pressed to justify fat fees for a job on which a crucial element of expensive advice – the pricing – has shown to be wrong. The brokers involved, too, will be sore. They will have put their clients into the issue, and they will be grumbling. All of the City professionals will have lost face.

There is more. Many companies come to market because a public quotation brings prestige, and makes day-to-day business dealings easier. Public companies are recognized as more substantial clients in any deal, more respected as tenants to rent buildings. Their customers and suppliers are influenced by dealing with a public company, whose standing is reflected in the share price. A successful flotation counts a great deal in image terms, and matters to employees who may be happy to buy a share in the business they work. Who wants to be with a loser?

If an issue opens below the flotation price, some investors will sell at once, taking a small loss and moving on. That selling may push the price still lower. As soon as it pulls back up to the issue price, other investors will want to get out at break-even, hampering any further advance. And if it goes higher, there will be the chance of selling by the underwriters, who never expected to be called upon to take up extra shares in the first place. The whole image will be smudged. Whenever City folk think about the shares, the first thing that will come to mind is that the flotation went wrong. It raises an immediate question mark.

There is, then, a mass of powerful reasons why any new company coming to market wants the float to go well. So the sensible tendency is to err on the side of caution in pricing, to give a little sweetener away. There are exceptions, of course: companies and sponsors whose greed gets the better of their common sense. There are companies, too, where coming to market is the one big hit for the promoters, their chance of making a killing, come what may. Such companies, happily, are few and far between.

MORE NEW ISSUE ADVANTAGES

Because most new issues are deliberately offered at a discount to entice new buyers, that fact, if nothing else, makes such issues a more inviting purchase than the average share. There are other pluses. By and large, companies coming to market tend to be in a more vigorous phase of growth than the average. They are hungry – perhaps even greedy – for gain and glory. They are floating because they are growing fast, and want money and prestige which will allow them to continue expanding. New issues tend to be newer companies, or established companies that have undergone a transformation and taken on a more vigorous attitude.

The average new issue chairman is out to make an impression on the world, ambitious for more fame and fortune. Never underestimate the power of the ego. Some folk make a fabulous living, tucked away out of sight, where no one notices what they are up to. Some swear it is much easier to do so out of the public spotlight. Coming to market changes all of that. The directors are on stage, their moves scrutinized by the City, examined by shareholders, hedged about by a massive new tangle of rules they could dodge when they were private. You do not go public for the fun of it. You do it because you want to see and be seen. Being labelled a success matters to the man who takes his company to market. And a public company with a strong share price opens up opportunities for expanding by acquisition, being seen to be still more successful, which are denied to those who have to rely on mere money by working in private. Such companies are not being floated with the idea of living with a share price that sits still. It may start a little low to lure investors in. But then the idea is to get it as high as possible, as quickly as possible.

Companies are forced to earn that chance the hard way. The process of coming to market is expensive and arduous, often requiring changes that in themselves force the company to become more efficient. No respectable issuing house will float a company without many months of 'due diligence', research to make sure that the company is in good enough shape to survive in the public arena, and can justify the claims being made for it. Often the bankers and brokers will insist on additional financial controls, weaker departments being beefed up. In the process, they will make the company stronger, while their continuing advice should help, at least in supporting financial skills.

All of this is good for the investor because it should ensure that there are no nasty surprises ahead. As ever, the system is not perfect. Shocks do happen sometimes. One or two newly-floated companies do miss profit forecasts. That means red faces and lost money all round for the City backers. In some cases, they have bought back shattered shares from the public to make good their mistake – a splendidly honourable solution. In others, the directors have been hauled over the coals, and sometimes forced to provide special deals to investors. In yet others, the sponsors have effectively turfed out the board, and injected new management and sometimes new businesses. No one wants a new issue scandal, and the City goes to unusual lengths to avoid it. It damages so many reputations and harms business in so many other areas.

By and large, the impact of all manner of City folk crawling over a company for months before the issue does tend to bring any dangers to light before the float, and to allow them to be sorted out in advance. Budgets and profit forecasts will have been examined time and again, and should hold water. The average quoted company has great scope for fudging things, dodging in-depth examination by outsiders. Few new issues get to market without the most thorough going-over, the likes of which they will never get again while the same management rules.

Going public is not something undertaken lightly, not something to do if the board wishes to jog along with the quiet life. Buying a new flotation on the main market, especially one sponsored by a house with a good reputation, means that the investor can be fairly confident there are no nasties in the woodwork, and that any surprises should be pleasant ones. The company will have gone through the wringer. Partly because of that challenge, it is apt to be more dynamic than the average – and a better investment.

BEATING THE MARKET

Absolute answers are elusive in the stock market because prices change continually, and so much depends on the market mood at any time. But the figures tend to confirm that new issues do, on average, outperform the rest of the market. The *Investors Chronicle* took a sample of the main market offers for sale in 1985, and reckoned that they beat all-comers by about 2 per cent – a pretty modest win. The story was much different for 1986, however. Offers for sale with full Stock Exchange listing then beat the *Financial Times* All-Share Index by 22 per cent. Only one in three failed to beat the average. Good or mediocre, all together rose an average 11 per cent in the first month – remarkably close to our projection that the ideal new issue should be priced at 10 per cent under the going market rate.

Surveying the 1986 new issue market in June 1987, the *Investors Chronicle* established that the *Financial Times* Actuaries All-Share Index had risen by almost two-thirds since the start of 1986. Offers for sale in 1986 outperformed the market by 18 per cent, making them a terrific investment. The average fixed price main market offer for sale added 62 per cent during the *Investors Chronicle* survey period – though some of them had not been on the market for much more than six months.

Even the first-time flops fared reasonably well, given time. The few new issues that were undersubscribed picked up strongly later. More than half outpaced the market, once they regained their poise.

Companies floated by tender, where the price is partly determined by investor demand (a detailed explanation comes in Chapter 3), did less well. They rose about quarter in the survey period, and lagged behind the average by 8 per cent.

On the Unlisted Securities Market, the Stock Exchange's company second division, the performance was almost as good as on the main market. Whichever way you look at it, new issues are winners.

A note of warning, however. No one should expect *every* new issue to be a winner, nor count on the stunning gains scored in 1986 and 1987 being repeated. It is possible, but those two years may prove to have been exceptionally good, even by the standards of an astonishing bull market that began to roar ahead from a black day in January 1975. New issues should beat the market in most years, but in a year when the market goes down, the average new issue might also fall.

There are no guarantees in the stock market. The stayers – investors who accumulate shares through new issues and hang on to them – may seem to have the averages on their side. But they will not escape the impact of a market fall. And at some point, what was once a new issue becomes just another share, one of the average investments, with no new magic. Inside the first month, perhaps, the new issue buyer reaps the benefit of the way the offer is under-priced. That should ensure an average 10 per cent plus on top of the general market performance. And over the first year or so, there is the benefit of being associated with a go-ahead company, anxious to impress as a public issue. Quite how long that impetus lasts is difficult to judge. But after six months, the new issue stayers really ought to examine their portfolio quite critically, assessing whether each share still has the positive virtues that make it worth holding, with the power to go higher. From that point on, what happens to the price will be determined by standard invest-ment criteria. It will need new buyers coming in to take it up. They will not buy because the company was a recent issue – indeed, they may hold off for a while to see if the prospectus promises prove correct. Building a portfolio as a new issue stayer makes a lot of sense, but with any share investment, the determined investor should never let it sleep. Constant re-assessment is the order of the day – as the Crash of '87 illustrated all too clearly.

13

3 The Joys of Stagging

The stag is the most spectacular animal in the Stock Exchange menagerie, moving faster and more elusively than the bulls – who expect prices to rise – and the bears – who expect them to fall. The stag is the investor who applies for shares in a new issue, hoping to sell at a profit as soon as dealings start.

Stagging has been a time-honoured and immensely profitable game through the centuries. Get it right, and it is a marvellous way of making money, with low risks and high returns. Where else can you put up £1,000 one day, and get back £1,860 a few days later, with the blessing of the government? All completely tax-free if you are a relatively small investor.

That is the way it worked with the British Telecom float, and that above all taught millions of people that there was easy money in new issues. Why bother with Premium Bonds if State sell-offs give you the chance of a big prize, and you get your stake money back before inflation has time to take a bite? Even if the prize is not so big, and the opening premium on the shares is small, or your cheque is sent back because you are unlucky in the ballot for a heavily over-subscribed issue, the game is wonderfully attractive.

When the stags are running, the whole process can gain a mad momentum. One issue attracts a large premium, so more money pours in for the next. The issue is so heavily over-subscribed that applications are scaled down sharply, and the stags get perhaps a tenth of the shares they applied for, with perhaps only a one-in-three chance in a ballot of getting anything at all. So in the next issue, the stags make ever-larger applications, knowing they will be scaled down and get far fewer shares than they seek. And they make as many legal applications as they can, and perhaps a few less-than-legal applications, trying to improve their chances in the ballot. It snowballs, and more and more money and more and more applications push over-subscriptions to ever more absurd heights.

It all becomes a crazy game, leading to something like the farce of

14

British Airports Authority float, where everyone who asked for more than £1,000 of shares in the fixed price offer – hardly a large amount – was eliminated completely, and got nothing. Successful investors were given a piffling 100 shares apiece. At the opening premium of 40p, that yielded a £40 paper profit, before dealing costs of £20 or more. For many, it was not worth the candle.

Even that farce, however, allowed the punters to walk away with their money returned intact, or a small profit. Not a loss. Even when it misfired, that stagging session left hardly anyone feeling sore because they were in the red. Once again, it illustrated how the odds are slanted heavily in favour of the players in the new issue game.

This book helps highlight some of the dangers. They do exist. The market mood changes. There will be times when stagging is no fun at all, when it changes from a low-risk punt to a dangerous and costly gamble. But while the government is eager to push ahead with a privatization programme, there should not be too much risk in the average State sell-off. The government has to pitch prices carefully. If one privatization flops, and costs the small investor money, the next one will be threatened. Once small investors get burned, they will fight shy of the next privatization. For the Government, however, a very great deal depends on a continuing programme of successful State sales. So, whatever the doubts and dangers, the odds are that they will continue to be worth stagging, though the temptation to tinker with the mechanics might make them less rewarding, as with British Airports. And BP? That was different. But no stag should have gone for it. The message that it would flop was plain for all to see – well in advance.

So long as the general stock market mood is at least mildly optimistic, stagging other new issues outside the privatizations should also continue to be rewarding. The scene changes all of the time. Sellers and buyers each become more wily, and the vast increase in the number of people joining the new issue game means there is much more competition for the same good issues, so the jam is spread more thinly.

If you fancy becoming a stag, though, do not be put off by occasional sneering references to the short-term, speculative nature of it. The stag is a gambler who need pay no heed to the waffle about long-term investment support for British industry.

Do not be fooled. There is no mysterious virtue in buying shares, holding on, and sitting with losses. Most of the City, no matter what the pretence, is eager for short-term gain. In classic theory, the greater amount of money flows to the most efficient businesses, where it generates the greatest return. Stagging follows that philosophy at its most aggressive. New issue sponsors need stags to create interest in share issues. If there was not sufficient support for British industry among other investors, then no one would be there to buy the shares from the stags, and give them a profit.

Traditional attitudes to stagging are riddled with hypocrisy. Never let anyone pretend that the whole tenor of the privatization promotion is not designed to welcome the stag. There are share bonuses for long-term holders of several privatizations. But the government knows there is nothing more alluring to the small investor than a quick, easy profit. And that many stags become longer-term investors in the end. Stags to the fore – your government needs you.

STAGGING ON BORROWED MONEY

Despite everything said so far to emphasize the risks in the stock market, and the need only to play with money you can afford to lose, it would be foolish to overlook the joys of playing the new issue game by stagging on borrowed money. This is what the market professionals do. So do many successful individual investors. Approached carefully, it can be highly rewarding, and need involve no serious danger of great financial risk.

Let me first, though, deliver a little lecture. In all of the investment books I have written, I have tried to make clear the risks as well as the rewards. As a financial journalist, I see too many stories of foolishness and gullibility among inexperienced investors. It can happen to you. If you are not careful, you can easily get carried away, and end up putting too much money into foolish situations. Any book on new issues which did not discuss sensible stagging on borrowed money would be ignoring one of the major opportunities. But please, please, please, do it sensibly. Please heed the rules I lay down. Do not get carried away. Do not think you have grown smart enough to stretch the rules. Disaster lies in that direction.

If you approach the new issue game as a stag, clearly intending to sell on the first day or two of dealings, it can make sense to be a little more adventurous with your finances. If you stick to companies that are being floated on the London Stock Exchange, where the rules are clear and well understood by everyone, and where there are high standards of integrity, you know it will be possible to sell any shares you get, on the published date for dealings to start. You may not know what price you will get, but the certainty of being able to get cash for the shares is invaluable. You do not have that certainty with shares outside the London Stock Exchange. If you are playing with borrowed money, ignore this type of share.

All being well, you will post your application form and cheque for your new issue, and about a week later, trading will open and you will be able to sell at a profit. In some cases, you will be able to walk into a stockbrokers' office, or a bank, hand over your allotment letter, and walk out with a cheque. The money you subscribed will be out of your hands, or your bank or building society account, for a week or two, at the most. And you will have it all back quickly, plus a profit. Terrific.

If the issue is a flop, you will still have been able to sell at once, and walk away with the proceeds. You may have lost a little money – but because it was a new issue, and the chances of a big loss are small, no great damage will have been done. Your stake money can go back where it came from.

If, however, you had been able to borrow money, and apply for twice as many shares, what would have happened? You might have got twice as many shares, and twice as large a profit if the issue had been a success. Or twice as great a loss if it flopped. Either way, because you could sell as soon as dealings began, and could get your stake money back so fast, you could pay off your borrowings quickly. Win or lose, the interest cost on the loan would have been modest, because the loan was open for such a short period. It adds a little to the cost of losing, but if you pick a winning issue, the profit on the extra shares you were able to buy using the borrowed money will probably comfortably outweigh the interest charge.

Take a simple example.

You have £1,000, and apply successfully for 2,000 shares at 50p each. You sell them for 55p – a profit of £100, minus dealing costs of £20, overall profit £80. Not bad on £1,000 in just a few days.

But borrow £1,000, apply for 4,000 shares at 50, and sell them at 55p. You have a profit of £200, minus dealing costs £35.30, minus interest charge £20, overall profit £144.70.

It could be even better. What if you had borrowed enough to apply for three times as many shares as you could afford? And got three times as many?

Borrow £2,000, apply for 6,000 shares at 50p, sell at 55p. Profit £300, minus dealing costs £54.45, minus interest charge £40, overall profit £205.55.

By borrowing on your £1,000 cash base, or 'gearing up' as they call it in the City, you have raised your profit take from £80 to £144.70, or to £205.55. In relation to your original £1,000 stake money, that £205.55 is very significant.

The example, too, takes a reasonable, conservative view of the possible opening premium, projecting just a 10 per cent gain. In recent years, however, that has often been too modest, especially on privatizations. The premium on British Telecom was 86 per cent, with 35 per cent on TSB, 67 per cent on British Airways, and 40 per cent on British Airports Authority.

Rework the figures assuming a 20 per cent opening premium – not, as the examples show, a wild assumption.

Investment £1,000, allotment 2,000 shares at 50p each. Sell at 60p – profit £200, minus dealing costs £20, overall profit £180.

Borrow £1,000, apply for 4,000 shares at 50p each. Sell at 60p – profit £400, minus dealing costs £39.60, minus interest charge £20, overall profit £340.40.

Borrow £2,000, apply for 6,000 shares at 50p each. Sell at 60p – profit £600, minus dealing costs £59.40, minus interest charge £40, overall profit £500.60.

The results are quite startling. By borrowing £2,000 on your original base of £1,000, you have made over £500, a terrific return. While dealing costs rise as your profit rises (I have assumed that the selling bank or broker charges a £20 minimum, or commission of 1.65 per cent on larger deals), your cost of borrowing does not rise. The borrowing costs are not calculated exactly, but are not out of line.

The examples are misleading, of course, because they assume you have been lucky enough to get all of the shares you have asked for in each case. In fact, if the issue goes to a 10 per cent opening premium, modest applications might well have been allotted in full. If the issue is successful enough to open at a 20 per cent premium, the allotment would almost certainly have been scaled down, so the profits would have been smaller.

Nonetheless, the examples do give the flavour of it. Borrow to stag, and you can ask for more shares at modest extra cost, and you are likely to get more shares on which to make a profit. If allotments are scaled down, you may well get more shares if you have been able to apply for more, so the borrowing still makes sense – provided you have done it carefully.

THE BORROWING TRAP

If the issue is a flop, and you have borrowed to buy more shares, your loss will obviously be greater. Rework the examples assuming that the 50p shares are sold at 45p, and the loss on £1,000 invested, nothing borrowed, is £120.

18

If £1,000 has been borrowed, the loss mounts to £200 on the shares, plus £29.70 dealing costs, and £20 interest, overall loss £249.70.

If £2,000 has been borrowed, the loss is £300 on the shares, plus dealing costs of £44.75, plus interest of £40, overall loss £384.75.

Clearly the cost of getting it wrong on borrowed money is high. If £2,000 has been borrowed, the overall losses wipe out more than a third of the original capital of £1,000.

It is worth doing the sums on a yet unhappier outcome, assuming the shares open at a discount of 20 per cent, or 40p, for a loss of 10p a share. On a straight £1,000 investment, nothing borrowed, the loss is £220.

If £1,000 has been borrowed, the loss is £400 on the shares, plus £26.40 dealing costs, and £20 interest, overall loss £446.40.

If £2,000 has been borrowed, the loss on the shares is £600, plus £39.60 dealing costs, and £40 interest, overall loss £679.60.

That gives a very different picture. Borrowing £2,000 on a heavy loser could wipe out a large chunk of the original £1,000 stake money. And if you have picked a loser, the chances are that you will get all of the shares you asked for, so the loss in the example will be the real-life loss. The only consolation is that very few new issues have opened at anything like a 20 per cent discount, and even a 10 per cent discount is unusually heavy. But it does happen, sometimes. Of course, you do have the option of leaving uncertain issues alone. The stickier ones are normally fairly easy to spot in advance, and if there is any doubt, there is no point in applying for them.

The message from the examples should be clear. Sensible borrowing to stag a new issue can bring rich rewards. As usual in the investment game, the extra reward is earned by taking on extra risk.

The cautious investor will want no truck with borrowing of any sort. Anyone more adventurous, however, will borrow, and judge their own prudent borrowing levels by reference to the stake money they can afford to lose. Taking on some borrowing can be consistent with the rule that you must not gamble with cash you cannot afford to lose.

You will not lose all of your stake money by stagging a new issue. Attempt to decide what losses you can afford before you make any borrowings, and act accordingly. The examples above show that, if you borrow twice as much as the stake money you have to lose, you should not come completely unstuck, even if the issue is a nasty flop. In the worst example above, a 20 per cent discount could cost you £679.60 of your £1,000. The detailed figures will differ in practice, but the example gives a good illustration of how it goes.

Borrowing need not be a trap if you are sensible. It can be a low-cost way of maximizing your stagging chances, allowing you to make applications for greater numbers of shares. As a rough rule, sketch out how the sums would look if the issue did go to a 20 per cent discount, and assume you got all of the shares you asked for. See how much of your stake money that would wipe out, and measure your borrowing capacity that way. There are no absolute rules, and you may feel inclined to stretch your borrowing muscle a little further for an issue that everyone reckons is a sure-fire winner. In general, though, be wary of borrowing much more than twice your stake money, that is, twice the amount of cash you can afford to lose. You simply never know what can go wrong – and if you do have a good run, and get it right a few times, you will be pleasantly surprised by the speed at which your profits boost your stake money, and allow you to expand your borrowing without taking too much risk. Start gently, and build carefully.

STAGGING SWIFTLY

One more special warning, though. The biggest temptation, once you have taken out a loan, is to keep it open. Never, never do it. It is easy to think that your shares might go better if you hold another day, easy to conclude that an extra day will add practically nothing to your borrowing costs, especially if it might boost your capital gain. DO NOT DO IT. Timing is the trickiest part of successful investment. No one can get it absolutely right. Some new issues open at a hefty premium, and quickly start to tumble. Others open slowly, and take off a few days later. It is very hard to predict how any one of them will go.

What is absolutely predictable, however, is that the cost of any loan will be ticking up day by day. The longer you keep a loan open, the faster you are heading for trouble. Do not load the odds against yourself. Borrowing to stag shares involves risks enough, without taking more chances. Every day that loan is open, the risks rise. Take the hit early. If a share you are stagging does not perform as you hope, get out fast. Settle for a smaller profit, or a smaller loss. If it did not do what you had hoped on day one, you have clearly misjudged it. Do not think you will judge it better on day two. You could be lucky – but it could get worse. You cannot afford the risk on borrowed money. The successful stag sells swiftly, and moves on.

THE WAY TO BORROW

Whatever you want to do, the rules might be dictated by someone else – your bank manager. Officially, banks are not keen on lending against share trading. When they do, they like customers to have investments to lodge with the bank as collateral, and will certainly be keen on some security.

It is worth asking, though, for a stagging facility. The banks know the score. They know stagging has been a profitable game in recent years, and that London listed shares are easily sold and turned into cash to repay a loan, so their money should come home quickly.

Much depends on how well you know your bank manager, but there is one useful piece of arm-twisting open to the better-off. Everyone around the stock market has their full quota of gold cards and such, the little pieces of plastic that offer a guaranteed overdraft, without the need for prior consultation. These are being given out ever more freely by banks eager to capture higher-earning customers. You need to earn £20,000 a year to qualify for most of them, but some are open to more modest earnings. Get one if you can – or mention the possibility of going elsewhere for one to any recalcitrant bank manager. You do not always have to be an established customer to get a gold card. Your manager will be reluctant to risk losing a good account for the sake of it. He may come up with one, or a stagging facility. After all, he will charge a fee for arranging the stagging facility, plus interest on the loan. He is in business to earn money by lending to his customers. You are doing him a favour by asking for a loan, not vice versa. Remember who is really the boss at your bank – you.

Unfortunately, there is not too much scope to raise stagging cash elsewhere. You can juggle with Access and Barclaycard, making only minimum repayments on some months, creating smallish amounts of cash instead of repaying monthly bills in full. But the benefit is modest, and there is not too much to recommend it. Once you begin postponing repayments, it is too easy to slip into longer-term debt. And that is certainly not to be encouraged for anyone who plays the share market.

MAKING UP YOUR MIND

Whatever you choose to be, stag or stayer, it makes sense to decide before you lay your money down. You can change your mind at any time once the shares are trading, and pull your money out quickly and easily. But you should not risk getting caught between two stools, starting as a stag, then lingering on and becoming a stayer. The

21

temptation is greatest when you go for an issue that does not yield as large a profit as you had hoped, or even goes to a discount. So you think you might hold on for a while, and then a while longer.

If you are doing it on borrowed money, you are simply being daft. If you can afford to take up the shares and sit with them, fair enough. But that will restrict the capital you have available for stagging other issues, if you started out as a stag. The techniques of selling are discussed in Chapter 11, but the clear rule is to cut losses quickly, and let profits run.

If you start as a stag, do not hang on to a disappointment, hoping it will come good. It may. But once you do hold on, the nature of your investment changes, and your approach should change with it. You need to be sure you checked what you were buying before you bought it. If you jumped in quickly because everyone thought it would be a runner, and did not check the prospectus properly, you need to go back and do it. Ask yourself why it has not proved as good a winner as you had expected. Maybe the market spotted something you missed. When you get down to reading the fine print, you may not be so happy to sit tight. And once you have decided to hold, you need to watch the price carefully, keep abreast of the market. A real investment stayer should commit more time and effort than the stag. You may not have the temperament.

So do try to be honest with yourself, and have your investment objectives clear before you start playing the new issue game. Make your decision, and stick with it. Stag some issues if you like, and stay with others. But try to do it by design, not by fluffing around. Unless you have a plan, given the astonishing reluctance of most investors to admit to themselves that they got things wrong, you will probably end up with a portfolio of lame ducks – shares you bought as a stag, which did not work out, and which you are just hanging on to in the hope of seeing your money back. It is a deadly undynamic investment philosophy and it happens, believe me. It makes no investment sense at all.

4 The Different Forms of Flotation – and How They Work

Whatever your objectives, to be a stag or stayer, you will soon see that new issues come in different shapes and sizes. They range from the fairly straightforward to the awkward and irritating, and to the downright impossible. Shares in some highly attractive companies can be written off as a new issue proposition because of the way in which they are brought to market. In others, most private investors are shut out completely, or the odds are loaded so heavily against them that the rewards are too slim to be worth the trouble.

THE FIXED PRICE OFFER

The staggability of any new issue is determined by a whole host of factors, but top of the pops for the would-be buyer comes the basic offer for sale at a fixed price. This is still the method used for most reasonably sized flotations. It offers the greatest scope for making a killing in new issues, because it forces the sponsor to earn the hefty fee he will be taking, and to pit his judgement against that of the market. When the sponsor gets it wrong, the issue either flops, or roars way to a hefty premium. The fixed price offer involves selling a chunk of shares at a price that is set in advance, before the market gets a chance to value it. No matter how popular the issue, no matter how many shares investors apply for, the selling price cannot be changed. Such issues are always underwritten to protect the company in case no one wants the shares, and to ensure that the company actually gets the money it is after, whatever happens. The underwriter is paid a small commission – normally between 1¼ and 1¾ per cent of the share price – in return for agreeing to take any shares left over after the sale. In effect, the underwriters get the shares at a small discount – if they get them. Most issues succeed, and the underwriters pocket their commission and move on to the next issue. If part of the issue is left with the underwriters, however, the opening market price is likely to be below the fixed price, and so the underwriters will show a loss. They will have to hold the shares, and hope they go better later, so they can sell at a profit.

Such niceties need not trouble the would-be buyer. All that matters is that there is a specific number of shares on sale, and terms will not vary. If the issue is over-subscribed, and would-be buyers send in cash for more shares than there are on sale, the issue is a success, and the shares are likely to start trading at a premium. There should be a profit for everybody. The greater the over-subscription, the greater the probable opening gain, assuming the market does not collapse between the offer closing and the first day of share trading.

If the issue is over-subscribed, the sponsor and the company have to decide how the shares will be given out. They have a fair degree of flexibility in this. Some companies will want to favour small shareholders, and will give a small number to all applicants, rationing them in a way that they hope will generate the most goodwill. A large shareholder list is expensive to maintain, with tens or hundreds of thousands of investors needing copies of the annual report and accounts, two dividends, and perhaps an interim profits statement posted to them each year. The State sell-offs have generally been eager to foster a big shareholder list, and to spread share ownership wider while seeking to generate goodwill. But already there have been rumblings about the need to reduce the cost of servicing so many shareholders.

Other companies prefer a smaller shareholder list, less costly to service, and concentrated among fewer, larger investors. When they ration out their shares in a successful issue, they will give larger quantities to investors who applied for more.

SCALING-DOWN

The favourite way of rationing is to scale down the number of shares allotted to applicants. This can be done in a variety of ways, but is rarely done by simply giving, say, half of what people wanted to everyone if the offer was oversubscribed twice. There will be cut-off points, and applications for up to a certain number of shares will get a certain proportion of the number they sought, with different proportions for applications of different sizes. That way it is easy to achieve the sort of shareholder list the company wants – lots of smaller holders, or fewer larger ones.

24

BALLOTS

Ballots – a lucky dip by another name – are also commonly used on heavily over-subscribed issues. Once again, the ballot can be fixed to favour larger or smaller applications. Frequently you will see that applications for, say, up to 500 shares go into a ballot for 100 shares, while applications for up to and including 1,000 shares ballot for 200 shares, and up to 2,500 shares ballot for 500 shares. There may be a certain superficial even-handedness about this. In the example, the upper limit on each bracket gets a fifth of the shares sought. In reality, however, the ballot is often not a simple one. It will be a weighted ballot.

The weighted ballot is another way of ensuring that the company gets a lot of small shareholders, or not. In the example above, it might be that a weighted ballot would give only one chance in ten of getting their 100 shares to those who applied for up to 500 shares, while those who applied for up to 1,000 shares might have a one in six chance of getting their 200 shares. And so on. Or it might be that those who applied for 2,500 shares will have one chance in two of getting 500 shares in the ballot, while others in the same bracket who applied for 2,000 shares might have only one chance in three of getting 500 shares, and those who sought 1,500 would have only one chance in four of their 500. Tricky stuff, but all part of the new issue gamble. There are no set rules.

CUT-OFFS

There are other variations. British Airports provoked controversy with a drastic cut-off point. Anyone who applied for more than 1,000 shares in the fixed price offer got no shares at all. One or two earlier issues had applied a cut-off point, giving no shares at all to very big applications – but no one had treated the small- to medium-size investor so rudely. No one got more than 100 shares. Hardly worth the bother.

Whatever the frustrations, though, of the way shares are rationed out under fixed price offers, these offers are the simplest for the new issue investor to operate, and do bring the greatest chance of reward. In many ways, they are also the fairest. Long may they survive.

THE OFFER FOR SALE BY TENDER

An offer for sale by tender enjoys flurries of popularity with issuing houses, but is generally not much fun for the stag, as it is still comparatively rare. It cuts the scope for big stagging profits, and if you are playing the new issue game for a quick hit, you may find it best to ignore tender sales. If you want to buy the shares as a longer-term investment, however, they can be worth considering.

Merchant bankers Morgan Grenfell used a tender for their own flotation, and pitched it so greedily that the shares never flew so high again until bid rumours got very serious. They used it, too, on Richard Branson's Virgin leisure empire, another limp performer. The State sell-off of British Airports also employed a partial tender which left little margin to make a quick profit. The message, unfortunately, is clear – tenders are heavily biased in favour of the vendor, at the expense of the buyer of the shares.

That is hardly surprising, since tenders are the investment equivalent of playing poker with an opponent who is allowed to see all of your cards before he places his bet. The most common form of tender sale involves the issuing house in advertising the particulars of the company in exactly the same way as a standard fixed price offer, but setting a minimum tender price at which the shares will be sold. The would-be buyer is invited to apply at the minimum tender price, or higher. In effect, the buyers have to say how much they will pay for the shares, above the set minimum.

The seller sponsoring the sale looks at all of the applications and the prices offered, and then sets the price. That is called the striking price. Almost every time, all of the shares are then sold at the same price. Anyone who has applied at or above the striking price will get some, perhaps with some scaling-down. If you bid below the striking price, you get none at all.

This means that if you are determined to get shares, you can tender at a silly, very high price, confident that you will be allotted shares at the same striking price as everyone else. If everyone pushes in applications at inflated prices, the seller will have enough applications at silly prices to sell all of the shares at a silly price. And everyone who went over the top will duly get what they asked for (and deserved) – wildly over-valued shares with the prospect of a loss when dealings begin.

That is the theory. In practice, no sponsor has so far been short-sighted enough to take full advantage of this. The sensible sponsor will not pitch the striking price at the highest he could get, taking the view that if he has ten million shares for sale, he sells only to the ten million who have made the highest offers. Instead, he will set the price below the maximum greed level, scaling down applications modestly, hoping to leave sufficient genuine buyers unsatisfied to ensure that there are enough would-be investors ready to buy at above the striking price, and so ensure a modest opening premium when dealings begin. Remember, in the new issue game, a premium is good for everybody. It keeps the issue smelling sweet, generates an air of success. No one with any sense wants to wring the very last penny out of investors – though some sponsors get tempted from time to time. They live to regret it in terms of reputation, and through the problems it brings them in later deals.

That said, because the sponsor – who is paid a hefty fee for advice on pricing, and then shuffles the responsibility off on to the investing public – is able to judge the likely demand before setting the price, he can be sure that he does not underestimate demand significantly. So the chances of a runaway premium in early dealings are eliminated. That speculative froth which ensures big stagging profits is siphoned off, in theory for the benefit of the company, or for the directors, if they are the sellers of the shares. By and large, offers for sale by tender are much less attractive to the stag.

GENUINE TENDER OFFERS

The tender routine outlined above is much the most common. But in the summer of 1987, a new and perhaps overdue variation appeared with British Airports – the genuine tender offer. In a sense, most tenders are phoney. Investors are asked to suggest a price they would pay, and then end up with shares at the same striking price as everyone else. There is no real reward for pitching your tender accurately. The clever investor who goes for a sensible price is no better served for his skill than the clown who tenders at a silly price, way over the top, and rides on everyone else's back.

In a genuine tender, the shares are sold at the prices investors actually offer. This happened for the first time in a significant UK issue with the British Airports tender. What you offered was what British Airports got. The tender for 100p part-paid shares was set at a minimum 142p. If you offered less than that, you got no shares in the tender. But if you tendered 150p a share – and many did – you paid 150p. And that meant you were showing a 10p loss when trading opened at 140p, while others with shares in the tender were only 2p adrift. No one would say what the highest tenders were. But it is certain that some, either through ignorance or folly, tendered at 160p or more, and were left nursing nasty losses.

So if you are tempted by an offer for sale by tender, be careful. Make sure you know whether you will be given shares at the same striking price as every other successful applicant – or whether the tender will be a genuine one, allotting shares at the price you bid. That requires a very special degree of care and attention.

THE MIXED ISSUE

British Airports was also the first sizeable offer for sale that mixed methods. A chunk of the shares were on offer at a fixed price, and duly yielded a juicy percentage profit for those who got them, though restricting successful applicants to 100 shares meant the actual profits were very small. Another chunk of shares were sold by the genuine tender, and left little room for profit.

The great Autumn 1987 sale of shares in British Petroleum also came with all sorts of knobs and whistles, distinguishing small investors from the big boys, and old investors from new. That one was all the more complicated because there were already massive numbers of BP shares traded on the market, with a clearly defined price, and so the Government had to try to devise ways of luring new people in on an old story.

For the dedicated new issue punter, BP scarcely qualified. One of the opportunities in playing the new issue game is the gamble of going into the unknown – you can never be absolutely sure what will happen. With BP, several forests are cut down each year to supply paper on which to debate every nook and cranny of the company's operations. At best, BP was never going to be a big short-term profit surprise.

Both BAA and BP illustrate, however, that the issuing houses are growing more inventive, devising more of a challenge to the would-be stag. So much comment, some of it ill-informed, about the profits to be made on earlier privatization issues has made the government more wary of giving too much away. But new issue pricing is a tricky business, and BAA and BP both came early in the life of the third Thatcher term. As the next election comes nearer, and as the search for convincing privatization candidates grows more difficult, there may be a change of mood. It will not be advertised, but it would be surprising if there were not more big give-away privatizations before the current programme comes to an end. BAA, especially, looked a little greedy of the government: BP flopped. The balance will eventually swing the other way, and pricing will be more generous.

Offers for sale mixing the issue methods, though, may become more common. They are a sure sign that the issuing house is trying to be greedier, to wring out a higher price for the vendor. That obviously makes mixed issues less attractive to the stags, and they should be approached with much greater caution. There is no point in taking any risks at all in new issues. Nothing says you have to play. If in doubt, stay out. When you get greedy, you get careless.

A PLACING

Often the most lucrative share flotations for the stags come with placings – if only the stags can climb aboard. In practice, you can only get a piece of the placing action if you are a big, favoured punter, or extremely lucky.

Placings are perhaps the most obvious example of how the Stock Exchange system – which is, by and large, constructed to appear to give most people a reasonable break – favours the boys in the market. Many smaller issues come to market as a placing, and most new issues on the Unlisted Securities Market use this method.

There is a fixed price offer for sale of shares in a placing, but only a small number of shares will be available, commonly between 10 per cent and 25 per cent of the issued capital. Three-quarters of them will be placed by the issuing house with big institutional clients, and other favoured investors. The rest may be offered to another broking house to place with their clients, and a small proportion will be made available to the market-maker.

Small investors used to have an outside chance of getting a few shares by asking their brokers to put their names down with the jobber (the old-style market-maker). Changes in the system in 1986 mean that even that slim chance has now largely disappeared. In practice, the simple stag can write off placings. The chance of getting any shares at the issue price are remote. In recent years, the bulk of placings have begun trading at a handsome premium, usually anything from 20 per cent to 60 per cent. Nice work if you can get it. If you do normally trade through one of the broking houses that sponsors a lot of USM placings, you might eventually wheedle your way on to their list, and be offered a few shares now and then. But there is no point in accepting an inferior service in other departments in the hope of such a distant dream.

INTRODUCTIONS

The introduction is another method of bringing shares to market, and another that can be written off as a simple stagging operation. Widely used by large overseas companies who want a London listing, this simply involves the company's sponsors signing up market-makers who will agree to trade in the shares henceforth. Such companies already have shares in issue, usually on an overseas market, and no new capital is for sale at the time of the introduction.

Sometimes the introduction sees a company stepping into the London Stock Exchange from an inferior outside market, either an Over-The-Counter listing, or perhaps some quiet matched bargain facility where occasional shares change hands between willing buyers and sellers. There are no straightforward new issue pickings for outsiders in introductions.

EARLY BIRD OPPORTUNITIES

For the devoted new issue chaser, however, it is wrong to write off placings and introductions completely. There are profit-making opportunities for early bird buyers. Especially placings often open trading at below the price they settle at a week or two later. The whole business can be extremely speculative, but anyone who is prepared to do their homework carefully in evaluating a placing stock can make a killing with a little nerve. Homework is crucial. Examine the prospectus, make up your mind what you are prepared to pay, and stick to it. Do not get carried away, and chase the price higher if it should roar away. Approach the task with a clear measure of the premium you are ready to pay above the original placing price, and do not exceed it. You may be pleasantly surprised how often you can make money that way, especially if you are buying not for a quick killing, but with a view to holding for six months or more.

The opening premium will be influenced by all sorts of factors, some of them unrelated to the basic investment merits of the stock. Many issuing houses will have a quiet agreement with the people who do get stock. There will be an understanding that shares will not be sold for the first few months or so, and may, indeed, be held for quite a while. There can be no official agreement on this, but customers who do not recognize the virtue of holding on to stock that they are allowed in a good placing may find they are not given the chance of future profitable issues. Sometimes, indeed, there may be a further understanding that anyone who has been given shares in a placing will buy more of them when they actually come to market.

Such unwritten understandings can only really work with placings because there are relatively few shares on the market. Buying power, and weight of money, can make a real impact. There is a chance of those in the know influencing events – sceptics might say 'rigging the market', though that would be unkind.

This can work very well for those who appreciate what is happening. It ensures that there is no great flurry of profit-taking when dealings start, and that there are guaranteed buyers around to take the price still higher – all unofficial, you understand. But a good sponsor will somehow see to it that those who appreciate the company's merits enough to want shares at the issue price will know that there are further money-making opportunities ahead in those shares.

Sometimes this means that the price in the first hour or so of dealings is very high, and stays that way, with little trade from buyers or sellers. Sometimes the opening price is so high that even the most sympathetic new investors take profits, and it falls back. There may be a buying opportunity then. On other occasions, the price will open at a more modest premium, with sales perhaps by some of those who got shares in the placing but for some reason have not been persuaded that there is more to come. A buying opportunity may then arise for the alert outsider.

You may be able to buy shares in a placing on the first day of dealings at a premium of 20 per cent or 25 per cent, and see them hit a 50 per cent premium within days. The appearance of shares on the market, and in newspaper price lists and comment, will attract more attention. That may bring in buyers, and the sponsoring house may be picking up shares for those who could not be satisfied in the placing. Usually the market will be fairly thin, and there will not be a large number of shares to be traded. So relatively modest buying orders can bring a sharp rise in the price.

Sometimes the opportunities can be rich indeed. In the summer of 1987, for example, brokers T. C. Coombs placed shares in an oil and gas play called Far East Resources. Those fortunate enough to get shares in the placing paid 80p. For a day or two, it was possible to buy at around 105p. A week or so later, it was possible to sell at 160p. Exceptional? Yes. Unprecedented? Certainly not.

A similar pattern sometimes emerges with introductions. It is important to distinguish between introductions of shares which have another sizeable market elsewhere, and introductions which bring a company to a proper market for the first time. Obviously if there are millions of shares already traded freely elsewhere, the chances of excitement are low. If, however, the company was previously stuck in a small, obscure, or unreliable market – such as the Over-The-Counter market – buyers could be attracted by the prospect of buying and selling on a properly regulated market with reasonable and reliable facilities for trading in volume.

Once again, such shares could start life at a hefty premium over their previous rating. A few have more than doubled instantly. But the early

31

bird might get the chance of buying at a premium, and still making a quick profit on the back of others who move less swiftly.

In the summer of 1987, for example, shares in Guidehouse, a small financial services group, were introduced to the Unlisted Securities Market by N. M. Rothschild. Originally issued in December 1984 at 26p, the shares traded on a matched bargain basis for some time. Ahead of the introduction, they were changing hands at 60p. When they hit the USM, they went to 100p on the first day, and later reached 135p. The Guidehouse example demonstrates that there are not just opportunities in chasing up introductions, but that there are also killings to be made in the wilder markets outside the Stock Exchange – if you know what you are doing.

5   Stock Markets – the Good, the Bad, and the Unspeakable

It is no accident that this chapter comes with a heading that brings a spaghetti Western to mind. There are many more bad guys out there in the assorted stock markets of the world than Clint Eastwood could ever send reeling, and many of the markets themselves are run with about as much law and order as the average town which The Man With No Name shot up. It is no joke. If you get careless trying to make a killing in the new issue game, you could well wind up flat broke and busted, buried in some investment Boot Hill, without a second chance.

Time and again, I have been brought up with a jerk by meeting some unfortunate who did not understand that all stock markets are not the same. There is not one great global stock market. There is not just one United Kingdom stock market.

It is easy to be deceived. There are too many sharp salesmen ready and able to take advantage of the unwary who assume that any passing reference to the 'stock market' or the 'Stock Exchange' means that they are dealing with that ugly great tower block in the centre of the City of London. That Stock Exchange is fine. But there are many others, and many of them are far from fine. They are extremely nasty, crooked places. Sometimes what a sharp salesman will call a 'stock market' is nothing more than the telephone he is talking into, the desk he is sitting at, and the printing press churning out worthless pieces of paper in the room next door.

At the risk of being a little unfair here and there, it is easy to advise would-be investors on where to go, and what to avoid. Simple. If you stick to shares that are applying for a listing of some sort on the Stock Exchange, London, safeguarded by the rules of The Securities Association, you can sleep relatively easily. Anywhere else, and you could be in trouble. There are markets in London, outside the Stock Exchange proper. They do trade shares. Some of those shares can bring great opportunities for profit. Others on the same market mean almost instant disaster. Yet other stock markets outside London – and

33

especially offshore – are little more than devices for stealing your money.

This message cannot be repeated too often. No matter how frequently I have sounded warnings through the years in the *Daily Mail* and elsewhere, I continue to hear from people who have been guillible, greedy and sometimes downright stupid, and fallen into the trap set by sharp salesmen – and now, sometimes, women. In this chapter, I attempt to set out the main differences between the different markets, and to suggest how you might make money outside the Stock Exchange proper, with a combination of good luck, good sense, and strong nerve. But if you are ever in doubt about any of it, stay out. Stick strictly to the main exchange.

THE STOCK EXCHANGE

It is easy to attack the Stock Exchange proper. Following the Big Bang of October 1986, when the rules were changed radically, the trading floor in the tower block in Throgmorton Street, close by the Bank of England, is no longer the centre of the action. The vast bulk of business is now done over electronic systems, screens and telephones, often from offices well away from the Stock Exchange building. The system is imperfect, the rules are constantly under pressure, and it can all be exploited quietly to favour those who actually work inside it, rather than the investors who approach it from the outside simply to buy and sell shares.

That said, the Stock Exchange is basically fair and honest, run by well-meaning people with a strong sense of responsibility. The problems attract attention because they are news, and news is a departure from the norm. Most of the time, the system runs smoothly, as it should, with nothing worthy of comment, and fair deals all round.

It is governed by complex rules which do not always produce the desired end. But the old motto 'My Word Is My Bond' still holds pretty well. Things do go wrong from time to time. Some investors are not always treated as well as they would like, or perhaps as well as they deserve. But the system is tried and tested, and works well enough for most people most of the time.

Like it or not, you have to accept that insider trading does go on in the London Stock Exchange, and on any stock market. No matter how tough the rules, how severe the penalties, greed will always tempt some to try and use privileged information to their advantage. If it outrages you on moral grounds, then stay away from shares. Insider trading will rarely act to your distinct disadvantage, and there is nothing you can do about it anyhow.

Significantly, the Stock Exchange has been ahead of the law in operating a compensation system to protect investors from abuse by brokers, the members of the Stock Exchange, and from the collapse of member firms. Pressure to cope with international trading on a 24-hour day means that the scale of everything is now very different, and the Stock Exchange is controlled by The Securities Association, which is responsible to the Securities and Investments Board with a rule book a mile thick, too confusing for any one mere mortal to understand, and all ultimately linked in to the new Financial Services Act. You can contact the Stock Exchange at the Public Information Department, The Stock Exchange, London EC2N 1HP (telephone 01-588 2355). They supply all sorts of valuable information – free of charge – on the rules and how they work. If you ever need a higher authority – and that is unlikely – The Securities and Investments Board is at 3 Royal Exchange Buildings, London EC3V 3NL (telephone 01-283 2474).

A FULL LISTING

You can feel confident of a high degree of fair play and integrity, then, in trading on the properly recognized stock exchanges which fall within the scope of The Securities Association. The main activity is on the Stock Exchange, London, but there are trading floors covered by the same rules and with the same high standards in Belfast, Birmingham, Bristol, Dublin, Glasgow, Liverpool, and Manchester.

Under the Stock Exchange umbrella, though, there are three different categories of share – those with a full listing, those on the Unlisted Securities Market, and those traded under the rules of the Third Market.

As the name suggests, shares with a full listing fall into the senior category. Companies with a full listing must show a trading record of at least five years before they qualify. When they come to market, they must offer at least 25 per cent of their share capital for sale, and the offer must be advertised quite widely.

Not all fully listed companies are big companies. There are many veterans that have fallen on hard times, and shrunk, or that simply failed to keep pace with the growth around them through the years. By and large, though, fully-listed companies are more mature and more substantial than the rest, and have more shares available for buying and selling. This can be crucial. When the crunch comes, the ability to sell a share matters more than the price. If the market in a share is poor – that means that it is only possible to buy and sell in small quantities

35

through only one or two market-makers – you are at the mercy of the market-maker. He can slash his price in times of trouble, or effectively refuse to trade, whatever the rules say. The bigger the company, the greater the number of shares in existence, and the more market-makers trading in them. The existence of several market-makers means that the price cannot be dominated by perhaps one dealer, and that there will almost always be someone willing to buy at some price, however bad the outlook.

The majority of fixed price offers for sale are of companies seeking a full listing. These are effectively the cream of the new issue crop, the standard stamping ground for the successful stag. There will be a better chance of getting shares, all else being equal, than in a company seeking another form of listing. It will be easier to sell at a sensible price, and the company, by and large, should be of better quality, and a less speculative investment than those floated elsewhere. If you are a cautious, conservative new issues fan, stick to fully-listed flotations.

THE UNLISTED SECURITIES MARKET

The Unlisted Securities Market – or USM – is the Stock Exchange's second division. It was launched in 1980 amid complaints that securing a full listing was just too onerous and too expensive. It came partly as an answer to the unregulated market in smaller company shares which was beginning to spring up outside the Stock Exchange. Companies coming to the USM need only a three-year trading record, and can sell as little as 10 per cent of their share capital. That has obvious attractions to ambitious directors reluctant to give away too much of a company which they think they will be able to expand quickly, but which would benefit from having shares to use to buy other companies, or as a source of extra finance. A flotation on the USM is also cheaper, and generally involves less advertising and red tape. Once again, though, there have been growing criticisms that the market has become over-regulated and too expensive.

For the would-be new issue buyer, the USM can provide rich pickings, but at a higher risk. USM companies are less mature. Some have missed their prospectus profit forecasts badly, and a few have gone bust quite quickly. Many, many more have gone on to produce impressive capital growth, and graduate to a full listing.

The biggest snag is that the majority of USM flotations are now carried out through a placing, locking the new issue punter out. Once again, though, investing on the USM takes you into a reasonably well-regulated and safe market-place.

THE THIRD MARKET

The Third Market sprang into life in January 1987. Like the USM, it was largely prompted by competition from unofficial markets outside the Stock Exchange. It is much the riskiest of markets inside the Stock Exchange, and may wilt if there should be a long period of falling markets, with a danger that Third Market shares could become hard to sell in reasonable quantities at reasonable prices. The idea is to offer a relatively cheap and cheerful way of allowing smaller, less mature companies to raise money by share issues, while extending to investors some degree of security by involving members of the Stock Exchange with their relatively high standards of integrity.

Each issue has to be sponsored by a Stock Exchange member firm. That firm is held responsible for keeping an eye on the company, and for trying to ensure that there is a reasonable market in the shares at all times. After a slow start, the market is beginning to gather steam, and the price performance of the early issues was generally good before the autumn '87 crash. As it grows more established, the quality of new issues may rise.

Again, several of the issues have been done through placings, but there are offer-for-sale opportunities. New ventures are allowed on to this market, and inevitably there will be failures. It is a market to be avoided unless you are prepared to take a high risk in the hope of higher returns.

BUSINESS EXPANSION SCHEMES

Some of the shares traded on the Third Market have been issued under the Business Expansion Scheme. This allows the investor to set the cost of shares in qualifying companies against income tax, effectively reducing the cost of shares by 60p in every 100p for those who pay tax at the highest rate of 60 per cent. The tax saving is lost if the shares are sold within five years, and the shares cannot be traded under a full Stock Exchange listing, or the USM within three years.

Some BES qualifying companies have performed extremely well over the short term, though there have been many well-publicized failures. This is not an area for the new issue punter, and no one should consider buying into a BES issue unless they pay tax at not less than 40 per cent and are prepared to tie up their money for at least five years. A few BES companies have issued shares that can be traded without the BES tax savings. Be careful. Some of these shares trade at the same price as shares that retain their BES tax savings – they should not. BES qualifying shares are worth much less without the tax advantage, and unless you buy those shares in the original offer – and not on the secondary market – you cannot get the tax savings. So if ever you think of buying into a BES company, you should look to pay significantly less than those who hold the parallel shares which carry tax concessions.

THE OVER-THE-COUNTER MARKET

By the time you read this, the Over-The-Counter market in the United Kingdom may be no more – but I doubt it. This market has developed outside the Stock Exchange among companies that originally needed only a licence from the Department of Trade. That all changes as the Financial Services Act comes into operation, but it has proved a moveable feast. It is conceivable that most parts of the Act will be up and running by the second half of 1988. If that happens, time could be running out for many of the best-known names in the OTC market. Under the Act, they will have to belong to FIMBRA, the Financial Intermediaries, Managers and Brokers' Regulatory Association (telephone 01-929 2711), or, more probably, The Securities Association if they are to continue making markets in shares as one of their main activities. Both FIMBRA and The Securities Association are making it difficult for OTC traders to gain entry, and without it, they will have to cease trading. By the time, however, that appeal procedures have been exhausted, we may be into 1989. And until then, the OTC heroes and villains can struggle on.

By then, many of the better companies that have been traded outside the Stock Exchange could have made it to the Third Market, or even the USM and respectability. As they do so, they are likely to yield useful profits to anyone who had the nerve to buy them earlier. Equally, it could well be that a number of better-established names will come in to make OTC markets, matching willing buyers with willing sellers. Or perhaps the big names who were struggling for acceptance in 1987 will, after all, find a way into the system.

Whatever happens, it looks as if the Financial Services Act will eventually add substance and respectability to the OTC market. But it will never make it the equal of any of the markets controlled by the Stock Exchange. OTC markets will always be more dangerous, and will feature shares whose prices move sharply up or down without apparent reason, and which may sometimes be well-nigh impossible to sell.

And those are the good ones. Despite repeated assurances of action, and endless good intentions, the authorities have proved dismally ineffective in weeding out the villains in the UK fringe markets through 1987. The Department of Trade has been especially lame, ignoring warning after warning in the press and from within the industry, about particular companies and market-makers. It would be nice to think things will change but it would be foolish to assume they will.

That makes it important to warn all but the most careful and calculating new issue punters off the OTC market. There are handsome profits to be made by the careful selection of OTC issues. Sometimes there are useful staging profits, with gains of 25 per cent or more in opening trade. More often, it can pay to spot a good company as it comes to the OTC market, and to sit with it for a year or two, waiting for it to grow enough to gain a place on one of the markets within the Stock Exchange. Then it will reach a much wider buying audience, and could yield substantial capital gains along the way.

MAKING THE CHECKS

Do not be tempted by shares in these markets, however, unless you are prepared to look very carefully at the prospectus, and to reject any but the very best. Do not stop there. Check with trading rivals, trade papers, brokers, anyone you think may help. And apply to Companies House for details of the individual companies that make up any new group. Ask around, too, for the trading background of any directors. Go to Companies House, look up the list of their other directorships, and get out the files on those companies to see how they have fared. Any question marks – auditors' qualifications and such – and you should walk away.

And do try to pick shares where there is more than one OTC market-maker. It may not always be possible. If OTC operators have a really good issue, they are reluctant to let rivals in to share the gravy, and if others do make a market, they rarely manage it in any size. But even if a second market-maker is more shadow than substance, any little extra dealing opportunity, somewhere else you might sell a few shares in an emergency, is useful on the OTC.

After all of that, be prepared to lose all of your money. No advance investigation can give you full protection against something going badly wrong in any OTC company, no matter how good it looks. Remember – if the company was that good, that convincing, it would almost certainly be able to find support enough outside the OTC market to hang on until it was good enough to creep in under the Stock Exchange umbrella, especially now the Third Market is expanding.

The OTC market is effectively the market of last resort. A few very good companies start that way. Rather more scrape out a living that way. And unfortunately, a high proportion simply go bust.

THE SALESMEN

Do not rely on any assurances you are given over the telephone by OTC salespeople. Ask by all means, but if any salesperson tells you how much profit you might make over what sort of period in anything they recommend, or how much the opening premium is likely to be in any new issue, put down the phone. They will be conning you. They cannot legally give you any guarantees. If they do, the guarantees will be worthless.

Whatever their training, few of them have any real understanding of what makes companies tick. The ignorance of some of them is quite appalling. Some are teenagers barely out of school. Others bounce from dodgy dealer to dodgy dealer, enjoying very high earnings for a short run. And they do tell lies. Whatever the system, they are well paid to sell shares to you. They want your money. Do not be impressed by suggestions that they need to make money for you to keep your custom. They will soon find another mug if you drop out.

Finally, do not be unduly impressed by evidence that the market-making firm belongs to FIMBRA. That is no guarantee. FIMBRA has been fighting a far better fight than many have given it credit for, but faces an impossible task in policing a mass of investment companies. Until the Financial Services Act comes fully into force, FIMBRA lacks the real muscle it needs. Even then, it may have too big a job to do. In the end, you are on your own. You make your own decisions, your own mistakes. Nobody can prevent you from being stupid – and only you will benefit from being careful and conservative.

OVERSEAS MARKETS

If the Stock Exchange proper is the good market, and the OTC the bad, the absolutely unspeakable markets are mostly overseas. Do not have anything to do with them.

No matter how good they sound, they are not for you. Smooth salesmen will tell you on the telephone that the Over-The-Counter market in America is a monster, biggest in the world, dwarfing the London Stock Exchange. It is a giant indeed, trading shares of some of the biggest, fastest-growing companies in the world, and the shares of some of the dullest, most obscure companies, the just-living dead. There are duds galore in America, traded on the splendid NASDAQ system. They sound terrific. Or what about Vancouver? There is a sizeable, lively market there, certainly. Plus countless tiny resources companies which exist in little more than name.

These are ideal hunting grounds for crooks. Many of the world's greatest share swindlers, supreme artists in the psychology of selling, come from Canada. They buy hundreds of thousands of shares in dud companies, paying perhaps one tenth of one cent for each share. They dress them up, print a glossy brochure, invent some exciting tale, and sell them over the telephone to gullible Europeans, unsuspecting Britons, for $5 each. The newer salesmen work from a written script, an answer on paper for everything you might ask.

And when the penny drops, and you want to sell the superstock you bought from them, you are told to hang on for good news, any day. And if you insist, the phone line goes dead. Or the salesman explains that his firm only sells shares, never buys. Or apologizes that there is no price today – try next week, and so on.

Those are the shares in companies that exist. Other crooks sell shares in non-existent companies, doing imaginary deals, just about to get a quotation on NASDAQ, or some other distant market. Forget them. Despite publicity galore about the Amsterdam boiler houses – high pressure selling teams pushing worthless stock over the phone, and stealing hundreds of millions of dollars before being kicked out – hapless investors carry on falling for the old tricks.

NEVER, NEVER, NEVER buy shares from anyone who is not a member of the Stock Exchange, or FIMBRA, or anyone who writes or telephones from abroad, or tries to sell you shares that are not yet traded. If you cannot see the price on an exchange in the United Kingdom which you know exists outside the salesman's office, forget it. No matter how they dress it up, how good the rest of the advice in the newsletter they send you seems, do not buy. You will lose your money – every penny of it. Why should a total stranger want to give you such a good deal, out of the blue? You would not buy used fivers from him for £2. Why buy phoney shares? Use your common sense. DO NOT LET GREED MAKE YOU BLIND.

6 How to Pick the Plums

The outline is clear. You are clutching cash you can afford to lose, you understand that a straightforward fixed price offer for sale in a company applying for a full listing on the London Stock Exchange is your best bet, and you are eager to make a killing in the great new issues game. Where do you start? How do you find out what new issues are on offer, and who is offering them?

It is not always easy. There is no simple, widely available list published where everyone can see each day. You will be bombarded by newspaper advertisements and television commercials for the big privatization issues, of course. It was impossible to escape the great hunt for Sid ahead of the British Gas flotation, and although the authorities pretended they wanted a lower-key launch for British Airways, you could hardly miss knowing about it, what with Concorde buzzing Buckingham Palace, and the Saatchi brothers giving saturation coverage with BA commercials on the small screen. For the British Petroleum sell-off in the autumn of 1987, millions of potential investors were sent direct mail shots through the post, inviting their interest. And the great advertising spending splurge ran riot.

WHERE TO FIND FLOTATIONS

Richard Branson broke new ground with television commercials for the flotation of his Virgin entertainments empire, but most new issues from companies outside the State sector do not get the advertising overkill. You have to hunt quite hard for some of them. The dedicated investor has to work at it, knowing that the flotations which attract the least coverage might be just the ones that yield the greatest rewards, simply because there may not be such a rush for them, and successful applicants might be allotted rather more shares than in the one that catches everyone's imagination.

There is absolutely no substitute for keeping your eyes on the financial pages of the daily newspapers. The *Daily Mail* often disregards some of the smaller placings, simply because very few readers will be able to get shares in them. But there are regular comments on the more attractive issues. Like all City pages, the *Mail* often gives advance warning of exciting issues well before they are due to be advertised. Watch, and contact the broking house or banker, if their name is mentioned. Ask them to put you on the list for a prospectus when one is ready.

The best record of forthcoming new issues is in that excellent weekly magazine the *Investors Chronicle*. That carries a special section devoted to new issues from the recent past, the present, and the future. There is also a newsletter *The New Issue Share Guide*, available by subscription from 3 Fleet Street, London EC4Y 1AU. It covers all new issues, advises on their attractions, and offers a phone-in advice line. It is fairly expensive, but is sometimes available on reduced-price subscription. It is worth taking for the dedicated new issue punter. Keep an ear open, too, for other telephone advice services commenting on new issues. They are relatively inexpensive – the cost of a premium rate phone call – and though some may not be totally reliable, you will soon learn which to trust.

GETTING A PROSPECTUS

Once you have found out what is on offer, you will need to get hold of a prospectus, the document that gives the full details of the company and the share offer, and carries an application form. That is vital. You must submit your applications on a proper form, culled either from the prospectus itself, or from a newspaper. Photocopies of application forms are not accepted.

You can get prospectuses from the sponsor of the flotation, usually a merchant bank or a stockbroker. Write and ask, or telephone. Some prospectuses are available in large branches of the leading banks, or sometimes from branches of the business whose shares are for sale. Tie Rack, for example, had prospectuses and application forms in most of their branches. Share shops, too, may have them.

Under Stock Exchange rules, prospectuses have to be advertised in full in some newspapers. The *Financial Times* carries virtually every prospectus, with an application form. The bigger, more popular issues are also advertised, with forms, in some other broadsheet newspapers, daily and Sunday, and sometimes in tabloids like the *Daily Mail*. Newspaper sales counters are used to bulk orders on the day a particularly popular issue is advertised. The sponsors often run out of printed prospectuses, and big stags find the cheapest and easiest way of getting application forms is to buy larger numbers of newspapers, clip the coupons, and throw the newspapers away. City waste bins sometimes overflow with cast-off prospectuses and newspapers when there is a big issue on the way. City litter levels can give a useful clue to the likely popularity of different issues.

THE MINI-PROSPECTUS

Partly in answer to this, issuing houses have begun to print a mini-prospectus for the most popular issues. This sometimes contains little more than the application form, and is either available from the issuing house or advertised in the newspapers. It is a cheaper, simpler way of providing application forms for those who have read the details elsewhere, and simply want to apply. In some cases, it suffices for stags who do not want to know the details, but are ready to apply blind, trusting to luck, or popular opinion, that the issue will be a success. They simply close their eyes, and leap aboard the bandwagon.

BUYING BLIND

Buying new issues blind like this is fine, so long as you realize what you are doing. You are taking a complete gamble, with nobody but yourself to blame if you get it wrong. In theory, everyone who applies for any new issue should read the prospectus carefully, evaluate the likely success of the company, and frame their application accordingly.

That is pie-in-the-sky for many people, especially with the great privatization issues. They do not read the documents but simply join in, knowing that previous State sell-offs have been big winners, and the next one should be the same. Politically, perhaps, they think the government could not afford to put them on a wrong one.

That may be naïve, and could go sadly wrong if the market turns down. In practice, it probably works quite well. So long as you appreciate the hit-or-miss nature of such an approach, good luck. But remember BP.

LISTENING TO THE EXPERTS

Taking it a sensible stage further, many people may prefer not to wrestle with the fine print, but simply to be guided by their stockbroker, or by their favourite newspaper columnist. I can hardly argue with that. Brokers and financial journalists should have the experience and training to tackle a prospectus, and to make sensible judgements. Many of them do.

Be careful, though. Some brokers will be passing on advice given by a highly skilled research department, capable of a far more informed judgement than most individuals can bring to bear. But others will be working for financial supermarkets who are involved in the issue in some way, either as co-sponsors (they should tell you), or perhaps as underwriters, agreeing to buy some of the shares if the issue flops. Or there may be other subtle links across the City that colour their judgement.

Financial journalists, too, are not perfect. Those on daily newspapers work under great pressure. They do not always have time, or perhaps the experience, to read all of a prospectus carefully, and think about it. They get things wrong, just like anyone else. Pick a columnist whose judgements you trust, and err on the side of caution, picking up any question marks in the newspaper comment. It is irritating how often adverse comments have to be framed carefully or obscurely. The laws of libel are a very real constraint on plain speaking, certainly in the City columns.

Try to follow comments by named individuals whose ideas make sense. Columns signed with pen names are often written by different people, with different abilities. And financial journalists move around a lot. The column may go on for ever, while the contributor who originally gave it a good reputation may be long gone.

THE GREY MARKET

The surest indicator of new issue success in recent years has been the grey market, the strictly unofficial market in new issues made by some firms outside the Stock Exchange. At times, they have begun quoting prices in new issues from the moment the prospectus has been published, so that it has been possible to get a guide as to your likely opening profit or loss before filling in your application form. Though there have been hiccups, on the whole such grey market prices have been a remarkably good guide, generally erring slightly on the conservative side. This has meant that, if an issue had an offer price of 120p, and the grey market price was 130p, you could be pretty sure of getting at least a 10p premium when dealings actually opened.

The game has become rather more difficult as the authorities have frowned ever more heavily on the grey market. There are now unofficial prices in fewer new issues, and the market may die as the Financial Services Act comes closer to operating. In any event, it has been more restricted, and sometimes has not opened until application lists have closed, making it no use as a guide to would-be applicants. By and large, the grey market only trades with professional investors in large size. Private investors should steer clear of it. It is no good selling shares in the grey market before you can tell whether you will actually have them to sell as a result of your application.

FOLLOWING THE CROWD

The grey market operators have had such a good forecasting record because they canvass the views of big investors on any issue before they start making a price – and then see how those big investors trade. To some degree, they are simply following the crowd, the best-informed crowd.

In a way, it is irritating to report that this is actually the surest indicator of new issue success. In the end, the number of applications, and sheer weight of money sent in, determines how any new issue fares. The weight of money is determined by the collective decisions of each individual investor, in theory after examining the prospectus and assessing the company. That most certainly happens with the big City investors, who may be underwriting the shares, as well as applying for them in the issue. They set the broad trend, and others latch on.

That broad trend is what matters most. If the big money reckons it is right, then it will be right – at first, anyway. Their sheer money power will make it work. If the big boys do not like an issue, it is much less likely that support from the public can make it a lasting winner, unless it is fairly small.

One way or another, the flavour of the decision by the big boys filters down the line. Brokers pick it up and spread it. So does the press. Usually it is possible to get the feel for an issue in this fashion, and that can be enough to rely on, worrying about nothing else. Buying blind, merely following the leaders through broker or press comment, usually works well enough. Sadly, stubborn independence is not always the best answer. You can work hard in forming your detailed judgement of an issue, and reach a firm, logical conclusion. But if that differs from the mass of opinion, you will be proved wrong – at least at the beginning. The weight of money matters most, and if you vote against that, you will lose.

THE BIGGER THE HYPE, THE GREATER THE GAIN?

The bigger the promotional hype, the greater the likely gain in the opening price. That is a dangerous line to follow, but it works, more or less. The Government certainly has faith in it. Senior privatization advisers have privately made very clear their view of the connection between how much advertising money they were spending, and how many shareholders they expected to attract.

Heavy advertising half-failed with Virgin – but that was an offer by tender. Some smaller issues have done wonderfully well, after a quiet promotion. But as a rough and ready rule, the more promotion, on television and in the press, the more likely an issue is to succeed, simply because it will pull in more money from more people. Again, it is the weight of money.

Similar observations apply to the company names we all know. With branches opening all across London, there was no shortage of moneyed investors who could see that both Sock Shop and Tie Rack were fast-growing companies, and decided that the shares might be good. A couple of years earlier, everyone knew the Laura Ashley name, and thought – rightly – that buying shares when they came to market must be smart. Wellcome is a name most of us know and respect, and a share success. TV-am had no shortage of viewers ready to buy shares. So long as the price was not pitched at an obviously greedy level, such well-known names were almost certain to succeed.

THE VALUE OF MAKING UP YOUR OWN MIND

Going along with the hip-hooray and bally-hoo can almost be investment policy enough to ensure a killing in new issues, then. Go for the big ones everyone says will be winners, leave the rest alone, and you will surely come out well ahead.

But there is a real value in making up your own mind, doing the hard work on the offer for sale document yourself, and acting out of your own conviction. It gives you a sense of satisfaction, of course, and should allow you to sleep easier. It will also help you to make money in a far wider range of issues, the ones that attract less attention, and the ones where not everyone is unanimous about the attractions. Those are the issues where a smaller response will mean that there are more shares to go round, and you are likely to be allotted enough shares to make a really worthwhile profit, if you get it right.

There is a reward for doing your homework on some of the popular issues, too. Perhaps the best example of this in 1987 came with the flotation of Tie Rack, which I touched upon in my introduction. Bigger than Sock Shop, whose shares had earlier opened at double the offer price, Tie Rack looked a sure thing until the prospectus came out. Then it emerged that the sponsors were seeking to sell the shares at more than 30 times earnings – a very high rating (I deal with such ratings in more detail in Chapter 8). The average store share was then selling at just under 20 times its earnings.

That was cheeky enough, and put off many experienced investors. They also hesitated to apply, knowing that Tie Rack would be so popular that the chances of getting many shares in the offer would be slim. The real cruncher, though, came in the fine print, tucked away in the back of a long and complex document. There it emerged that just under half of the shares would be owned by a Swiss trust, which was controlled by people who were not identified. They had no intention of causing any problems, the document suggested, but there they were.

Such a large share stake meant that these mystery investors effectively controlled Tie Rack. It was in their interest to see that Tie Rack continued to prosper, but, in theory at least, they could call the shots. Nothing the sponsors could do to emphasize how reasonable the whole thing was could explain away the misgivings of some commentators. In fact, the full offer for sale document was not made available to the press when they met the company directors. Some newspapers never read the document properly later, and never commented on the mystery share stake. Those that did were uneasy.

In the event, Tie Rack shares attracted a massive oversubscription, but never put in the price performance to match. Offered at 145p, they touched 200p briefly in early dealings, and then began to slide. A few months after flotation, they were below the 145p issue price. There may be a time to buy at that level. But for the new issue game, too many big investors had stayed away, and too many applications came from punters seeking a quick profit. The high asking price, the lack of support among influential brokers, and the unsettling Swiss stake all took the bloom off what looked a sure-fire soaraway success. The casual punter who bought blind might have been left holding when the price tumbled. The stubborn individual investors who took the trouble to read the fine print, and make up their own mind, would have had doubts all along. Perhaps it was worth a quick punt. But only a quick one, and then away.

7   How to Read the Prospectus

You can duck delving through a prospectus, and still make a killing in new issues. But the serious player, and anyone who plans to make regular forays into the new issue market, really ought to learn their way around a prospectus. It may seem daunting at first, but once you know where to look, and how to look at what you find, it is amazing how quickly you will feel able to make sensible judgements about investment. And you will soon find that a little intelligent application allows you to swing the chances of making money more consistently your way.

The Stock Exchange stepped in and clamped down on glossy, photo-filled offer documents just as they began to grow popular a while back. In their sober-sided style, the officials worried that inexperienced investors would equate pretty pictures and livelier presentation with investment merit, and might be led up the garden path by slick shadows, rather than substance. There is some merit in that view, but it is a pity that prospectuses have been forced back into a boring mould. Photographs of what the company does really could be rather useful. These days there are products and processes galore that baffle most of us when explained in technical terms. A picture sometimes made it a whole lot easier to grasp.

If you can, get hold of the prospectus document itself, rather than the one in the newspapers. The newspaper version will be complete, but the fine print is usually much more difficult to read. And many of the trickier bits are in the smallest print, as you might expect.

The opening pages of the prospectus tell you the name of the company being floated, and the sponsors, and explain how many shares are for sale at what price. Many prospectuses now have a page near the beginning giving a brief outline of the essentials. Study it. It is easy to get lost in the body of a bulky prospectus, and find you have read some sections without really understanding the basics you need to put them all into perspective.

THE ESSENTIAL OUTLINE

The outline you need to grasp is which sponsor is selling how many shares, at what price, to raise how much money, and who gets it. You also need to know what proportion of the issued capital is for sale, what value the issue puts on the whole company, the size of the latest profits, any profit forecast, what the dividend yield is at the issue price, and what price earnings ratio the shares are being valued on.

Most of those figures will be in the summary at the front of many offer documents. If they are not, it might be handy to make a note of them as you read through. All of them should crop up somewhere.

WHAT SPONSOR

The sponsor is usually a City merchant bank or a stockbroker. They will generally have been advising the company for many months, perhaps years, on how the business should be shaped to make it suitable for flotation. They may be lending the company money, and may have bought some shares themselves at a lower price along the way.

The bigger the name of the sponsor, the better. Established and respected City names really do know how to do these things best. They know the routine, are familiar with what big investors expect of a public company, and will generally ensure that all of the professionals involved are top class (and expensive). The big boys have the contacts to ensure that institutional investors will be properly briefed about the merits of the company, and will pull all of the strings they can to get their support, which is essential for a real success. Any nasty surprises should have been smoothed away. Any tricky problems should have been tackled well in advance of the flotation: difficult subsidiaries sold, loss-makers closed, skeletons raked out of cupboards, maverick directors made to understand how they should behave. The transition from private to public company can be traumatic. It involves a radical change in style for most companies. They do need very firm and clear guidance. And the big boys know how to do that best.

The reputation of the issuing house will be on the line as much as the company itself. No City house likes to be associated with a dud. The biggest names can pick and choose. They have less need to cut corners, less need to try to get away with floating companies that may not quite be up to scratch. Big name backing is no absolute guarantee of merit, but it really is a help.

Unfortunately, deciding just which big names are the best has become much more difficult in the last couple of years. The highest flyers of all, Morgan Grenfell, came a nasty cropper over the Guinness affair, and have been associated with some limp new issues – most notably Virgin and their own flotation. Hill Samuel, another bank in the top bracket, started to fall apart in the summer of 1987, while there have been problems bubbling beneath the surface in other houses since the Big Bang in October 1986.

As a rough rule, however, the top ranks still include the likes of Kleinwort Benson, S. G. Warburg, N. M. Rothschild (J. Rothschild is a notch lower), Robert Fleming, Lazard Brothers, J. Henry Schroder Wagg, Samuel Montagu, Hambros, Morgan Grenfell, Hill Samuel, Charterhouse, Barclays Merchant Bank, Lloyds Merchant Bank, and County Bank. Second-rank bankers include Singer & Friedlander, Brown Shipley, and Guinness Mahon.

The foreign invasion has changed the names of many of the best stockbroking sponsors, giving them greater cash resources, but leaving question marks over how their style of operation will develop. As a very crude guide, it seems that brokers backed by European houses have been upgraded by their parents' purse-power, and may be taking useful initiatives in medium and smaller companies. The formidable American money machines are showing signs of over-aggressive pricing, or, to put it more bluntly, plain greed. The Japanese have yet to make an impact in new issues. If they do, their usual ploy of underpricing in order to win new business may yield opportunities. Once supreme among stockbrokers, Cazenove have taken a desperate bashing over the Guinness affair, but can still have muscle enough to get almost any new issue away, though they do tend to set prices on the high side.

Cheque-book power has been shaking up the City so fast that it is dangerous to be too dogmatic. Whole teams of experts are being lured from long-established houses to try their hands with total newcomers. Today's star could easily be tomorrow's dog. Clear guidelines are hard to set out. But, in spite of everything, the longer-established and more substantial names have a knack of surviving. There is no substitute for experience, and though newcomers may effectively buy their way into positions of influence, and surface with some excellent new issues, in the long run the safest houses to follow will be those who have been at it longest.

HOW MANY SHARES

The more shares for sale, the better. That means there are more to go around for everyone, and the bigger the company, the better and safer it will normally be. Bigger companies tend to be longer-established, and longer-established companies tend to have a more secure background.

WHAT PRICE

The actual price of the shares is relatively unimportant in isolation. Obviously investors prefer a 'light' price, one pitched under £2, rather than a price up in the £5 range. The significance is psychological. People like to feel they are getting more for their money. It always seems better to buy 1,000 shares at £1 each, than just 200 for £5 a time.

You can have too much of a good thing, however. Accounting tricks allow a company to pitch the share price at almost any level when it comes to market for the first time. There is no reason why, for example, a company should not float one million shares of £1 nominal value at £5 each to raise £5 million, or ten million 10p nominal value shares at 50p each to raise the same £5 million. The nominal value of a share is largely an accounting exercise. It has no great significance. All shares in United Kingdom companies must have a nominal (or par) value. In practical terms, it makes little difference to real value. You could as easily find a share bargain by paying £2.50 for a share with a 5p nominal capital as you could by picking up a £1 nominal value share for 5p. Do not let nominal values bother you.

Obviously this flexibility in fixing the nominal value can be used to create more shares to sell in the offer, and the sponsors will try to use this to ensure that the package looks attractive. Several major privatizations have been constructed to pitch the initial price of the shares at between 100p and 150p. That does not look too lightweight, but does give the buyers the feeling of getting a reasonable number of shares for their money.

Even British Petroleum had a scrip issue a while before their autumn 1987 sell-off. At well over £3, the shares were still on the heavy side then, but that was much better than double the price a year earlier. Being asked to pay nearly £7 a throw would have frightened off many smaller investors.

A word of caution, though. Penny shares have been all the rage – investors large and small love them. With that firmly in mind, some sponsors pitch their offerings way down low, just to attract penny share punters, knowing that many of them will buy purely on the strength of the price, paying no heed to investment fundamentals. So approach any low-priced issue with extra care. The fact that it is low-priced will probably ensure a good following, but it is unlikely to be as secure and well-founded an investment as something pitched at a chunkier price. Like so many guidelines, this one is a generalization, and may prove a little unfair to some sponsors and some issues. But the broad notion still holds good. Approach any flotation with a share price of under 60p with real care. It will almost certainly bear above-average risks.

HOW MUCH MONEY

The amount of money being raised in the offer for sale is obviously important. The figure will appear in the summary at the front of the document, or can be worked out easily by multiplying the number of shares being sold by the price. The more money the merrier, is in a sense, best for the stag, because there will be more shares to go around. A bigger issue will attract more of the big investors, who will buy for the long term, and will not be taking profits quickly in early dealings. And there will generally be more bally-hoo to attract more prospective investors.

On the other hand, some of the smaller, quieter issues can be more rewarding. The stag might get more shares, and big buyers might be unsatisfied, and come into the market to top up their holding when dealings begin. Scarcity value might help. Obviously, you have to be careful about a small issue getting overlooked at a time when one or two big ones are getting a great deal of attention. That might open a great opportunity for anyone ready to buy and hold a while, but may dampen the chances of a big opening premium.

WHO GETS THE MONEY

More important, though, than the amount of money being raised is who gets it. Sometimes all of the shares being sold come from the board and the people who have backed them. They are all cashing in, taking the money themselves. Even though some of the vendors may be staying on to run the company, and keeping a chunk of the capital themselves, this is not a good sign.

Everything is relative. If the vendors are taking a fairly small proportion of cash out through the float, and remain significantly committed, then all is well and good. But, whatever the reason given for their sale, deeds matter, not words. If they are selling a sizeable chunk of their shares, their commitment to the company is being reduced. The shares they keep will be saleable once the company is on the market (check the fine print to see what undertakings there are about future share sales by the board and big investors), and the directors can borrow against them, and use them in all sorts of ways.

The sale by a big shareholder who is not involved in the management may, however, be good. That may simply show someone cashing in on an early investment, and may perhaps remove a constraint on the management, who might have had to run the company while looking over their shoulder at their big backer. Circumstances vary. But check to see why anyone is selling.

Most frequently, a flotation will involve the people behind the business selling some shares, unlocking capital in what may be their only significant asset, while taking the opportunity to raise extra new money to expand the business. No one should begrudge board members taking some cash out, but obviously the fewer shares they sell, and the more new money raised, the better. Commitment to growth is what you want to see. Many smaller companies come to the Unlisted Securities Market precisely because it allows the directors to get quoted paper to use for expansion without selling many of their own shares, because they believe so strongly in the future of the business. You will be able to use your own common sense to judge what seems a sensible balance in the light of the explanations the board offers. Treat those explanations with a little scepticism.

THE AMOUNT FOR SALE

All of this is linked closely to the proportion of the company being sold. That will be larger with fully-listed companies. Once again, there are no hard and fast rules. If only a small proportion of the capital, say 25 per cent or less, is up for sale, there could be a limited market in the shares. That will make selling them more difficult, but could make them rise more quickly if they do go up. Generally, the board and their backers will want to release a smaller proportion of a good thing, if they are convinced it is going to go places. The stag, though, wants the chance of getting more shares.

Sometimes there is already quite a wide spread of shares among family shareholders, and others who may have backed the business earlier. They may be numerous, and may hold relatively small blocks of shares individually. Be careful if the fine print does not show that they have given undertakings to hang on to the shares for a year or more.

THE VALUE OF THE COMPANY

It is always highly instructive to check what value any flotation puts on the whole company. If it is not shown clearly, simply multiply the number of shares in issued capital (the authorized capital will normally be greater, but only the shares actually in issue count) by the price. It is a simple check, and is generally accorded much less significance than other measures of value used in the market. It can be quite an eye-opener, however. It is surprising how often the market value (or market capitalization) of a company can bring you up with a jerk. It is all too easy to grow accustomed to City jargon without really questioning it, only to find that an otherwise interesting investment proposition turns out to be valued at two or three times – or more – than you had realized.

This would emerge anyway in a careful examination of the various figures, but they can so often be dressed up differently. It is remarkable how often market value gets overlooked in a rush of enthusiasm, especially for lower-priced shares. Time and again I have met investors who complain at cautionary remarks about a company, only to discover that they have no idea that their favourite business might have assets of £5 million, and a market value of £60 million because it has far more shares in issue than they had ever imagined.

Market value is a simple figure, an absolutely invaluable reference. It should be crucial to every investment decision, and should come early in any discussion of value. There is nothing like comparing real asset worth with the market rating, nor the capital value with what may sometimes be puny profits. Would you pay £80 million for a company making £500,000 or less, and with assets of under £10 million? You would be astonished at how many investors would – unwittingly – because they never thought to check the market capitalization.

8   Making Sense of the Profits and the Fine Print

Sooner or later in the new issue game, you get down to looking at company profits. They are crucial, of course, if you intend to hold the shares for any length of time. Without a reasonable profits record, or the hope of higher profits, no company would be able to come to market. Ultimately, the anticipation of profits is what moves share prices – though, as we have seen, there is a whole lot else to worry about, too.

THE PROFIT FORECAST

The profits that are published in the front of the average prospectus may not quite be what they seem. Sometimes they will be historic profits that were made in the company's last trading year. Sometimes they will be prospective profits, the profits that the company is promising to make for the year which is in progress, or may just have ended. It is important to make sure you know which is which.

It is a cardinal City sin to fall short of the profits forecast in an offer for sale document. It happens rarely, but it does happen, and most often among the smaller companies, those that come to the Unlisted Securities Market, the Third Market, or the Over-The-Counter market.

Increasingly, the bigger flotations come shortly after a company's year has been completed, and the profits are in the bag, either fully audited or so near that any forecast is as good as the real thing. There is unlikely to be a forecast of profits from the company until most of that year is over. Look to see what the directors say in the section about prospects. They will be wary of too firm a promise, but there should be some suggestion that things are going up. Do not automatically assume, if they say nothing, that the way ahead is brighter. It usually will be – but every now and then, a company sneaks in to raise new cash in a dull year, and short-term prospects may not be too smart. Offer documents are worded very carefully, written and re-written by teams of experts. They are not often guilty of accidental omissions. If something you might expect is not there, it has been left out for good reason.

The chaps in the City will get a firm steer, however, from the company's brokers. Often the broker to the issue will send out a detailed projection of future profits along with the prospectus, effectively making a forecast without the company putting its own name to it. The practice is widespread and time-honoured, and has the advantage of keeping the right people in the know, without giving any guarantees.

Rarely, however, will the average new issue investor be able to gain direct access to that forecast. It is worth trying, however, either by contacting the sponsoring broker, or by getting your broker to find out for you. If the broker to the issue does not have a forecast, some other friendly house may well have made one to help things along. Often the financial press will pick these up and carry them in any comment. If the newspapers do give profit projections that are not in the offer document, you can be sure that they have come from brokers close to the issue, acting on a strong steer from the company itself. It is just another of the little ways in which the City professes to treat all shareholders equally and finds a way of making sure that some are more equal than others.

THE PROFIT RECORD

What you want to see is a record of strong profits growth, preferably sustained by any forecast, official or unofficial. The prospectus for a full listing will have a five year record of profits in the fine print. There will be a three year record for USM issues. The best show steadily rising turnover (or sales, effectively the same thing), and equally steadily rising profits. Past performance is no guarantee of the future, but it is about the best guide you will get.

Watch for exceptional items. Anything that is not a genuine repeatable contribution should be viewed with suspicion, and knocked out – profit from selling properties, or share stakes, for example. There should be clear explanations of any profit setbacks, closing loss-making factories, selling dud subsidiaries, and such.

Look, too, to see what the trend of profit margins has been. You can work these out simply by dividing turnover by pre-tax profits. A relatively new business may start with low margins as sales build up, and see them widen as more business is conducted on the same overheads. Margins may lurch around as extra capacity comes on stream, and new investment pays off. Be suspicious of any company where margins are drifting lower.

Clearly a profit record that dips and soars must be treated with reservations. The company may be in a volatile trade, and unless there is a very good reason to show why not, there could be a danger of similar fluctuations in future. Be wary, too, of companies where profits have leapt in the year or two immediately ahead of the flotation. You will need convincing that the higher profits are sustainable, and that the directors are not seizing the chance to sell shares while the going is good.

THE PRICE EARNINGS RATIO

The freshest profits figure will generally determine what price earnings ratio the shares are being sold on. The price earnings ratio is the City's most widely used piece of jargon. Variously known as the PE, the PE ratio, so many times earnings, or so many years' earnings, it gives a measure that can be used for a rough comparison of the worth of different companies.

Effectively it indicates how many years it would take for the company to earn its own market value in the profits that are available to pay out to Ordinary shareholders – that is after taxes and dividends due to any Preference shares. So if a company has a price earnings ratio of 12, it would take 12 years for that company to make profits enough to equal the value of the company as determined by the price of the Ordinary shares (very roughly the market capitalization, though strictly speaking that should include the worth of other forms of capital as well as just Ordinary shares).

It is all linked into the way profits are often expressed as earnings per share. You calculate earnings per share by dividing profits after tax and Preference dividends (if there are any) by the number of issued Ordinary shares. For example, if a company makes profits of £500,000 after tax and Preference dividends, and has an issued capital of one million Ordinary £1 shares, it has earned profits equivalent to 50p a share. If you divide the share price by those earnings, you see how many years it would take to get back the share price in company profits. So if the company earning 50p had a share price of 450p, it would take nine years (450 divided by 50). That is the price earnings ratio – nine.

Don't fuss if this all sounds a trifle technical. You do not have to know how to work it out. The figure will be in any prospectus, in most newspapers, and at the fingertips of any broker. Just ask.

It is important, however, to understand how to use the price earnings ratio. By and large, a high price earnings ratio indicates that a share is highly rated. Investors are prepared to wait more years to see their investment back, or – more realistically – expect that company to grow more quickly than the average, and so earn much higher profits quickly. A low price earnings ratio generally indicates expectations of slow growth.

As a crude measure, the way to tell an under-valued share from an over-valued one is to spot a company with a lower price earnings ratio than others in the same line of business. Obviously not all industries grow at the same pace, so different companies in different industries attract different ratings. For example, in the Autumn of 1987, the average brewery share sold on a price earnings ratio of just over 16. The average publisher sold on more than 28. New technology is bringing massive cost savings, especially to newspapers, so there are high expectations of fast growth for publishing companies. Merchant banks, in disarray in the Autumn of 1987, sold on less than eight times earnings – before the Crash.

Make the comparisons by scanning the share price tables in any of the newspapers that carry a column with PE ratios. Or turn to the stock market report page in the *Financial Times*, and hunt through the table of the FT-Actuaries Indices. These carry the average ratios for different sections of industry, together with the market averages and such. If you have spotted a PE that is way out of line with the rest, there will almost certainly be a special reason. The market rarely gets ratings completely wrong. But you will have something to get your teeth into, a reason to find out more about what is going on.

In truth, the whole thing is rather hit-or-miss. Obviously every company has problems and opportunities of its own. No two businesses have exactly the same outlook and attitudes. It is in distinguishing between those differences, and spotting opportunities that others have missed that the chance of making a profit in share trading arises.

Making up your mind about the right price earnings ratio is important in assessing the merit of a new issue in standard investment terms. But there is one extra trick to watch. The price earnings ratio at the issue price that appears in many prospectuses will be based on the forecast profits, if there is a profit forecast. That is not strictly comparable with the figures in most newspaper tables, or the FT-Actuaries averages. You must make up your own mind how much this matters. Smaller and newer companies especially often float on a forecast of sharply higher profits. Go to the profits record table in the back, seek out the earnings figure, and calculate the price earnings ratio at the offer price on historic profits. Sometimes you will get a shock. You may find that the company that looks reasonably valued on a prospectus PE of 20 is actually being floated on a historic PE of closer to 40 – think about it.

THE DIVIDEND YIELD

The other standard City measure of investment merit is the dividend yield. This, too, will be loud and clear in the prospectus. Usually it will be based on a forecast of the dividend the directors would have paid had the company been public for a full year. Like the price earnings ratio, you do not need to know how to calculate the yield. It is a simple way of telling you what return you would get in dividends for every £100 you put into the shares – rather like interest on a building society or bank account, except that it should rise as profits in the company grow. Or, of course, fall if profits collapse.

The main value of the dividend yield is again used as a means of comparing different shares in different companies. Broadly similar companies should be rated on broadly similar yields. An above-average yield means that either the shares are cheap, or the market is expecting poor profit growth with little chance of higher dividends – or even a reduction. A low yield shows that fast growth should lie ahead.

COVER

You may also find a reference to 'cover' or 'dividend cover'. That shows how many times company earnings (profits after tax available for distribution to Ordinary shareholders) exceed the cost of the dividend. A cover of two means the company has earned profits sufficient to pay the chosen dividend twice over. Cover of 1.5 means it could be paid one and a half times over. Cover of anything below one means that part of the dividend is being paid from reserves – not something you should come across in a new issue. Broadly speaking, the more cover, the better.

9   Watching the Way the Money Goes

At the risk of sounding deeply cynical, your favourite new issue may look perfect by all conventional standards – but when you comb the prospectus, there is no substitute for watching how the money flows to see if it all really makes sense.

Most in the investment world are decent, honourable people, ready to give everyone an even break. Until that conflicts with their own interests. Most of the time, the conflict does not arise. The system works smoothly, everyone pulling together in roughly the same direction. In my book *How To Make A Killing In The Share Jungle* (Sidgwick & Jackson, £5.95), I warned that everyone you come across in the investment world has an angle. So long as your interests coincide, and you both want to see the price of the same share going up, then all is well. In most cases, there is no reason for anyone you deal with to give you anything but fair treatment.

For every share bought, though, there has to be a seller. The conflict of interest is as fundamental as that. Everybody is aware of it, though it is easy to overlook. It is possible for there to be a happy buyer and a happy seller in the same deal with fair play all round. But there are levels and degrees of light and shade in it. Some deals are fairer play than others. Some judgements are coloured a little more than others. And every now and then, someone really tries to take advantage of the system. It happens everywhere, not just in the stock market.

The safest approach to share buying, then, is to be constantly on your guard for what other people may be trying to do. And there is no surer way to an investor's heart than through the wallet. When you think about buying a new issue, trace how the money flows around the sellers, the directors of the company.

DIRECTORS' INTERESTS

Read your prospectus carefully. Study what the company does, and what the chairman says about the way it does it. Are the company and the management experienced? Are they in an expanding industry? Or is it going ex-growth? Be especially wary of a one-product company, or a company heavily dependent on a small number of customers. Is it going public so that the business can be built more rapidly, or is it seizing the opportunity to cash in on a fashion for such companies?

Are the directors simply cashing in? Why are they selling any shares at all? Why come to market? Life as boss of a thriving private company has many advantages, no outside shareholders to worry about, no need to explain things, no one to query what expenses are charged on the company. There has to be a pretty powerful reason to abandon all of that.

You should already be aware of much of this from our earlier discussion about who gets what when the shares are sold. Carry it a stage further. If the company is family-controlled before and after the issue, is there the necessary commitment to further growth? Or is it just a nice way of raising capital, and staying locked in to a comfortable way of life with the extra prestige of a public listing, plus the higher value that that puts on the business – and the crucial facility to sell a few shares as time goes by?

Check the fine print carefully for undertakings about when or whether the directors can sell. If there are none, they may be able to dribble them out quietly. That may stop the price rising too much. Look at the kind of service contracts that the directors have. Have they given themselves fat contracts running for a long time? Watch especially for rolling contracts. Some of them run for five years, rolling over constantly. They mean the board are very near unshakeable, and would be entitled to massive compensation if anything went amiss and they faced a successful challenge to their position.

Ideally, you want a company where the people running it have a substantial share stake, but one that is not large enough to allow them to ignore the influence of other shareholders. Something less than 50 per cent with the board is best, though in smaller companies, an aggressive and ambitious boss may want to keep much more.

Check the fine print for share options. Are the directors able to get extra shares in return for better performance by the company? Options are good for everyone, provided they are not too generous. The general guideline is to allow the board up to 5 per cent of the capital in options.

There could be more. In some cases, you may find some board

members have sold businesses into the company being floated. They may be entitled to more shares if the company achieves certain profit forecasts. Such things are generally good news. Try to work out what profit targets have to be met for directors to get how many shares at what price.

Look, too, at the material contracts that always appear near the back of any prospectus. These will show what bits and pieces the directors have sold into the company, and what they have taken out. Clearly the prices in any such transactions are important. Have companies been sold in at inflated prices? Or assets taken out? Do these contracts suggest that the directors have another business on the side? Have they taken it out because it has good prospects? Or bad ones? Will it take up much of their time and energy?

Now and then, there are notes about cars, yachts, and aeroplanes. Many private companies have them. There is nothing wrong in it. They are normally bought out of the company before it goes public. Some of the comings and goings might give you a flavour of how the directors live, how they behave.

THE AUDITORS' REPORT

There may be more clues in the auditors' report. Ideally, this should be the most boring, routine piece in the prospectus. It should signify that the affairs of the company comply with the provisions of the Companies Act, and that the accounts represent a true and fair view. Anything else, and you should watch out. The auditors are accountants technically employed by the shareholders to ensure that the company's figures are what they should be. There is great flexibility of interpretation in this. But any qualification can be a serious matter, especially if the auditors do not also say that the matter they raise has been treated in a fashion of which they approve.

You can rest assured that if there is any reservation, any qualification, in the auditors' report, it is there with good reason. Companies hate to have such a thing, and will usually bend over backwards to avoid it. Major new issues are not normally floated with reports that are qualified significantly by the auditor. But this does happen sometimes with companies on the USM, and frequently occurs with OTC companies. It may also crop up in Third Market listings.

The most common such qualification suggests that proper records of stock were not always kept in earlier years. It happens frequently in fast-expanding small businesses, and need not always be a major worry. But it did crop up, for example, in one OTC company where a partner in an accountancy firm was a main board director. That appeared a remarkable oversight on his behalf. Sure enough, the company later collapsed. In itself, the auditors' reservation had not been very serious. But, perhaps, it gave a clue to the sloppy way the company was run. Perhaps that was a factor in the later collapse.

While you look at audit reports, give a thought to who the auditors are. Big firms are expensive, and do get involved in scandals from time to time. But they are best if you are backing a new issue. They should ensure that the company has proper accounting systems, which in itself will help the company prosper. Small, obscure firms of auditors should be viewed with caution. Sometimes they can be persuaded to bend where they should not. A public company account can mean a lot to a small auditor. If you have means of telling, avoid companies audited by tiny firms, or ageing partners – though those sort of things will only come up in OTC issues.

10   Application Tactics

Once you have perused your prospectus and decided which new issue to go for, how do you maximize your chances of getting the most shares to make the greatest profit?

The first step is to rustle up as much cash as you can to back your application. Very broadly speaking, the more money you can afford to put into applications, the better your chances of being allotted more shares. Bully your bank manager for an overdraft, but only if you realize you are taking an extra gamble by using borrowed money, and only so long as you are firm in your resolve to sell as soon as dealings start. If you are planning to use cash stashed away in the building society, talk to your branch manager first. On some big privatization issues, some societies have special arrangements that do not cost you so much in lost interest for shares you may never get. Some have even linked with stockbrokers to allow you to sell shares in the big issues over their counters. That has advantages. Check before you start.

MULTIPLE APPLICATIONS

Gone are the days when your cat or your goldfish could be a successful stock market stag, with their name on false multiple applications which would win them an allotment of precious shares for you to sell. By now, everyone ought to know that multiple applications are illegal on government privatization issues. The conviction of Keith Best for British Gas multiples shattered his career as an MP.

On the state sell-offs, sophisticated surveillance schemes linked to computers and operated by specially trained teams of accountants threaten to unearth even the most ingenious multiples, and have put an end to the cottage industry where City slickers used to employ pensioners to fill in forms, write cheques, and stuff multiple applications into envelopes. Some multiples probably do get through, even now. But the game is not worth the candle. If you are caught, you could end up in court, disgraced, and deprived of your profits. Do not even think of it.

The picture is not so clear on either issues, outside the government sales. Unless the prospectus says that they are illegal, and threatens prosecution, multiples may not matter much. At worst, they may just be destroyed. Some issuing houses will just turn a blind eye. Read the fine print; make up your own mind. But do be careful. Attitudes are changing – by the time you read this, the situation could be different.

In practice, though, a little gentle multiplication is still acceptable. Never make one application when two could do, if you keep it in the family. Married couples should apply separately as husband and wife, even if only one of the partners is really interested. And it is permissible to apply on behalf of your children. Read the application forms on how to do it. Most of them set the procedure out very clearly.

APPLICATION RINGS

Until recently, you used to be able to go further. Some people still do, and in most cases they will get away with it. It is difficult to stop people forming a little local co-operative, a kind of application ring, persuading friends and neighbours to allow them to apply on their behalf, perhaps in return for a share of the profits. They should be sure, though, that everyone knows exactly what is going on.

Strictly speaking, it is illegal in state sell-offs, and against the rules in others. The fine print on application forms varies, but basically in signing the form, you will be undertaking that this is the only application you have made for your own benefit. There is nothing to stop you filling in a form on behalf of a friend who is on holiday, and has asked you to help out, so long as the shares and the benefit from them do go to that friend. In practice, it is difficult for the issuing house to know exactly what is going on. Ten different people might make applications, and they might all be using money lent them by one person, and might give up some of their profits in return for the use of the money. Obviously if the ten names all bear cheques drawn on the same account, the sponsors might start asking awkward questions, if they notice. And it could all end in tears.

In practice, only the privatizations and perhaps the biggest issues are likely to be policed with such a careful, detailed surveillance. Other sponsors might not take such trouble, might even be glad for the extra applications. But you never know. It would be irresponsible to suggest that you should become involved in any form of unofficial application ring. Apart from the dubious morality of it, the possible rewards are hardly worth the risk of discovery.

TWO ARE BETTER THAN ONE

These days, however, it is clear that two small applications are better than one larger one. Any half-decent issue is over-subscribed, attracting applications for more shares than there are to sell. Most scale applications down, giving people fewer shares than they ask for, and often they hold a ballot to decide who gets what. Two applications instead of one double your chances of getting something. Four applications, one from each member of the family, young or old, are obviously still better.

NATURAL BREAKS

You can also improve your chances of getting more shares by studying the natural breaks that sponsors create themselves on their application lists. Typically, a sponsor will invite applications for up to 1,000 shares in lots of 100, applications for up to 5,000 shares in lots of 500, and applications for more than 5,000 in lots of 1,000 shares. In doing so, the sponsor creates natural breaks. It is not always so, but when it comes to allocating shares in a heavily oversubscribed issue, the sponsor may use those breaks as cut-off points.

In this way, he might allot 200 shares to those applying for up to 1,000 shares, 400 to those applying for between 1,500 and 5,000 shares, and 1,000 to applications for 6,000 and more. Clearly it makes sense to apply for the smallest possible allocation above each cut-off point. In that way, while anyone applying for 1,000 shares will get 200, someone going one step up and applying for 1,500 will get 400 – twice as many for an application just 1½ times greater. The same sort of thing holds good higher up in the example. Someone seeking 5,000 shares would get 400, while anyone going one step beyond the natural break level would get 1,000 shares by asking for 6,000 – a much better success ratio.

Obviously there are all manner of variations on this in practice. It does not always work. Sponsors create different cut-off points to those on the application form. But it has worked often enough in the past to make it worth looking at. It might give you a modest edge.

CHECKING THE FORM

It is worth taking great trouble to read the application form, and to complete it correctly. It sounds silly, but many applications are rejected because the forms are incomplete, or incorrect. The biggest mistake is applying for incorrect numbers. So when you look for the natural breaks mentioned above, be sure you follow the instructions. It is no good asking for 1,100 shares when the form says you can apply in lots of 100 up to 1,000, and lots of 500 thereafter. And do take care to sign the application form, and your cheque. And to cross the cheque, if it says so.

BONUS SHARES OR VOUCHERS

Everyone will have their own reasons to choose between bonus shares or vouchers if they are given the opportunity in privatization issues. If in doubt, opt for the bonus shares, even if you intend to sell right away. You never know, you might change your mind and hang on.

REGISTERING EARLY

In the same way, it is worth taking advantage of any special facilities offered with privatization issues. If you are able to register in advance for an information pack, or take advantage of a promise of guaranteed allotments by registering early, then do it. There is nothing to lose. You are not committed. You can always forget it when the time comes to post a cheque.

Do not, however, rely totally on being registered in advance. Every such issue brings a hail of complaints from people who did not get their information packs or application forms in time to apply, even though they signed on early. If time is ticking away, use an application form from the newspaper. It does not matter if you have registered already. What matters is that you do not make more than one application in your name. Early registration will not count as an application.

EMPLOYEE OFFERS

If you work for the company that is coming to market, you may well be offered some privileged position in the issue. If you are not, ask why not. These days, the Government is strongly in favour of worker participation in share schemes, and any half-decent company ought automatically do something special for employees when it comes to market.

Take whatever you are offered, unless you think the company is a dud. If that is so, you ought to think about changing your job. Some flotations give employees the chance of free shares, or extra shares linked to however many they buy. Others give the shares at a discount to the issue price, or set aside a certain number to meet employee applications on what are sometimes known as pink forms. Those pink employee priority forms are sometimes traded among spivs on the fringes of the Stock Exchange, bought by punters eager to ensure that they get shares somehow in a popular issue. Alternatively, employees will sometimes be approached by outsiders eager to lend them money to help them to apply for the maximum number of employee shares in return for a part of the profit.

Obviously anyone involved in pink form trading is bending or breaking the rules. Behind the scenes, one or two companies have taken tough action against employees who got up to such tricks, effectively firing or fining them. Do not do it. It is perfectly legitimate, however, to go to your bank, building society, family or friends to see if they will lend you money to finance a big application where you are offered special facilities as an employee. Almost invariably, it is worth backing such opportunities to the hilt.

Equally, it is worth joining any Save-As-You-Earn scheme that lets you buy shares in your company. These carry tax privileges, and often have a built-in safeguard against loss which makes them absolutely first class.

BY POST, OR BY HAND?

Despite the queues that sometimes trail outside receiving banks in the City on the morning of a big issue, most applications are sent in by post. It makes sense. Provided the post is working normally, and you allow three clear days for delivery, there is no reason why the application should not get in on time.

The danger, of course, is that sending off your cheque three days early leaves you exposed to the general market moods for that much longer. The climate does sometimes change sharply over a matter of days. Rarely does it change sharply enough to turn a winning issue into a loser, though a sharp market setback could turn a possible big profit into a smallish one. Anyone who sent their BP application off a week early lived to regret it.

Standing in line on the last morning does protect you against late shocks. But if you are not there bright and early, you might find the bank doors are shut at 10.01 a.m. before you have got to the front of the queue. For most people, hand delivery hardly seems worth the trouble.

Whichever way you do it, once you have parted with the form and your cheque, you cannot change your mind. You are committed. It is no good trying to ring up and withdraw your application, no good trying to cancel your cheque. You cannot do it. You are on the hook, for better or worse. So make sure you get it right first time.

APPLICATIONS CLOSED

Application lists normally open and close within a minute. Most will open at 10.00 on the morning listed in the prospectus, and will close at a token 10.01 a.m. Any applications in before 10.01, even days before, will count. An announcement that the lists have closed will be sent to the Stock Exchange. If the issue is a big success, it may say the issue was oversubscribed, or heavily oversubscribed. There will be no more detail at that stage. If the list does not close at 10.01 a.m. – rare these days – it means the issue is struggling, although once or twice sympathetic sponsors have kept the receiving bank doors open a little after 10.01 a.m. to allow late-comers to get applications in.

ALLOTMENTS

There will often be an indication in the next morning's newspapers of how much cash the issue has attracted, how heavily subscribed it was. There may even be an outline of how the shares will be allotted, or whether there will be a ballot, or applications will be scaled down.

Bigger issues obviously take longer to sort out. Sometimes it takes two or three days to count all of the applications, and work out the basis of allotment. It will be published in the press, and from that point on there may be guesses of the opening price reported in the City columns, or perhaps available from your broker, if he has time to talk to you. If there is an unofficial grey market, it will be operating by then, giving a good guide on the likely price.

FIRST DEALINGS

First dealings on the Stock Exchange normally begin about a week or ten days after the application lists close. The dates are given in the prospectus. Allotment letters, telling you how many shares you have got, are normally posted the day before dealings begin. It is an unsatisfactory system. Postal delays often mean that many do not know how many shares they have, if any, when dealings start. Those who leave home early may miss the morning's post. Sometimes it can take two or three days before allotment letters arrive. On some major privatizations, dealings have begun as allotment letters are sent out – a shoddy procedure that can put the small investor at a disadvantage to the professional, who by then can be sure how may shares he has, or who will have been guaranteed stock. BP, where they got everything wrong, traded for more than a week before allotment letters went out.

It is possible to get an advance indication of how you have fared in a ballot by going to your bank and checking whether your cheque has been cleared. If so, you should have been allotted the number of shares appropriate to the size of your allocation. That is not, remember, always the same as the number you applied for. But you can probably assume you have got whatever allocation was published in the newspapers for your application bracket.

Whatever you do, do not assume that you have got shares, and sell before you receive the allotment letter. Something could have gone wrong. Your form may have been lost in the post, you may have filled it in wrongly, or there may just have been a muddle. If you do sell and later find you did not get shares, you will have to buy them in the market to make good your sale, and that could prove expensive.

Your allotment letter should come with a return cheque for anything owing to you if your application was scaled down. If you have been unsuccessful in the ballot, your cheque will not normally have been cashed, and will be sent back around the same time as the allotment letters, perhaps a few days later. If you drew a cheque on your bank account, you have lost nothing in interest by failing to get shares, though it could have cost you a fee to arrange the overdraft. If you withdrew money from a building society account, you may have lost interest, although some societies have special arrangements to cope with this.

SHARE CERTIFICATES

If you sell at once, you will have to sign your allotment letter, and deliver it to your selling agents, the bank or broker, or whatever. They will want it, even if you sell only part of your allocation of shares. They will process the paperwork to make sure you keep what you want. Hold on, and you will eventually get a share certificate, several months later. The allotment letter, though, is a legal document, giving you title to the shares. Guard it carefully, because it is transferable. If it is stolen, the thief could sell it for cash. He will not be able to turn share certificates into cash so easily.

11   Taking Your Profits

All of your problems may appear to be over once that allotment letter comes tumbling through the letterbox, telling you how many shares you have got in the latest soaraway stock market success. Terrific; all you have to do is check the price, multiply the premium by the number of shares you have, and there is your nice, fat profit. What a wonderful business it is, especially this privatization programme. How super to see all of these growing companies coming to the stock market, spreading profits to investors all around.

Do not let me spoil the picture. It is as simple, or very nearly as simple, as that. Playing the new issue game is exciting and can be richly rewarding. Great fun for everyone.

Joining the share-owning democracy, though, does bring certain problems, certain responsibilities, and the odd worry or two. One of those infinitely enviable folk who had made a million or two once had the temerity to suggest that the getting of it was the easy part. The difficult job was to know what to do with it, or, more importantly, how to keep it.

The chance to worry that way would be a fine thing for most of us. But once you make your first killing, you will soon begin to appreciate that there is a problem or two you had not foreseen.

ARE QUICK PROFITS BEST?

No matter how seriously you have taken the warning that you should decide in advance what you want – a quick profit or a longer investment – once you actually have the shares and the prospect of a profit, there will be a temptation to stay. Having found such a good thing, why quit at the beginning? Surely if the stock market is prepared to put such a high rating on the shares, and give you the chance of a big profit at once, you must be on to a good thing? The City must know something. If everyone is rushing to buy, are you doing the right thing by selling?

Everyone in the market knows the old story about leaving a bit in for the next chap. The best traders may not make the biggest profit each time, but they do make a profit. They might not buy at the very bottom, but they do buy well below the top. Everyone knows, too, that the market overdoes everything. The rises are too high, the falls too steep. But when everyone else is rushing in one direction, it is hard to stand firm, and push against them.

That way, though, is the way to investment success. Do not be swayed by fashion. Do not rush along with the crowd. Make up your own mind, and stick to it. If you are determined to take a quick profit when you send in your application, do it when you get your allotment letter. Never mind that the price goes higher. So long as you have made your profit, that is all that matters. You will never hit the very top by anything other than pure luck.

That said, new issues generally tend to yield higher profits if held over six months than if you turf them out in half an hour. They have tended in recent years to yield still higher profits if held for a year, or 18 months. A few have multiplied four or five-fold inside a year, leaving those who took a 50 per cent profit on opening day looking rather lame. Or are they?

The debate cannot be resolved conclusively. So much depends on the general trend of the market. When the market is rising strongly, almost any share will show a greater rise the longer it is held. It is common sense. The stock market hit bottom in January 1975. By early autumn 1987, it had risen thirteen-fold. It rose nearly 50 per cent in the first half of 1987. Against that background, almost any half-decent new issue had gone on up beyond the first-day premium.

Look what happened, though, when the market slumped in mid-October. New issues followed everything down. The longer you hold a share, the longer you are exposed to the risk that the whole market will tumble. Any person who promises you that the market is going in one direction or another is simply guessing. The guess may be well-informed, or foolish. But you should place little faith in anyone, no matter how impressive, who predicts the market's mood more than six months ahead. Do not let the gobbledegook fool you.

The longer-term investor in new issues also has to ponder the opportunity cost of sitting tight. Is a 25 per cent profit in one day worth more than a 40 per cent profit over six months? Or a 50 per cent instant profit worth less than a 75 per cent profit over a year? There may be a way of getting an arithmetical answer on paper. But churn it around inside your head, and it feels like an impossible sum to calculate.

And what if you opt to hold on and do see the 75 per cent profit? Could you have used the money better to chase two or three more new issues, and clinched a 25 per cent profit on each of them? Would that have been smarter?

Anyone who traded through the great stock market slump of 1973 and 1974 was inclined to be itchier. They knew profits could vanish fast, with little warning. They knew the market could go down as well as up. Then came the Great Crash of 1987. Blind panic and plunging prices.

I traded through 1973, 1974, and 1987. It may have made me too easily inclined to snatch at profits. I have had to school myself against it. You must make up your own mind. But let me emphasize that every day you hold a share is an extra day on which you are exposed to the risk that it will go down. It might go up, but you cannot take the stock market for granted. The day you stop watching and worrying could be the day you are in trouble.

WHERE TO SELL

When you decide to take your new issue profits, the best place to sell is through a member of the Stock Exchange, your bank, or a building society. It may not be the cheapest, easiest way out, but it will be the safest. Share shops are fine, so long as they are operated by a member of the Stock Exchange, or a big-name High Street bank. The chain being built up by the Burton Group in branches of Debenhams promises to be ideal – available, efficient, and trustworthy. Stock-brokers Quilter are also building a chain of share shops that should do well.

Some brokers, banks, or building societies have special arrangements on selling new issues. You can walk in with your allotment letter, and walk out with a cheque. The major privatization prospectuses sometimes carry a list of brokers willing to sell at a low commission rate. You might find yourself paying a minimum commission of anything between £15 and £30. That can take a big bite out of profits if you have only been allotted a few shares. Never mind. Far, far better to deal with an expensive agent you can trust than a cut-price merchant who will leave you worrying about whether you get any of your money back. That is a bitter lesson I know many people have learned the hard way. Time and again, after every major issue, I field calls from people who have tried to save £5, and ended up losing £500 – or much more. It can happen to you if you are not careful, believe me. Do heed any warnings that appear in the *Daily Mail*, or elsewhere. And remember that the laws of libel do restrict what the press can say. Sometimes the warnings have to be couched in very careful language. Take the hint. If there is any criticism at all, no matter how mild, it may be that the newspaper concerned is trying to sound a warning, but there is a lawyer close by, monitoring every word. Better safe than sorry.

COMMISSION-FREE SALES

The pattern of the problems is totally predictable. The unwary investor has been attracted by some advertisement offering commission-free selling of a recent big new issue. The advertiser will normally be a member of FIMBRA, or still operating under a Department of Trade licence to deal in securities. Neither of these bodies is able to guarantee that all of their members behave as they should. The dealer will give an instant offer over the telephone, or may take allotment letters over the counter. The price offered may be a penny or two below that offered on the Stock Exchange, but because there is no commission or extra dealing cost to pay, the seller may end up getting just as much for the shares as by dealing with a stuffier Stock Exchange member, or at the bank. So far, so good.

If the seller takes the money, and has nothing more to do with the dealer, all is well. No harm is done. Most such dealers, however, offer commission-free trading in order to get the names and addresses of investors, knowing that they will be interested in shares, will have cash from selling the recent issue, and will often be inexperienced in investment.

The dealers then use the names and addresses to try to sell other shares. Sometimes these will be perfectly respectable offers of shares in companies quoted on the Stock Exchange. The dealers buy big blocks of them at a discount, break them down into smaller lots, and sell them to smaller investors at the full price, thus taking a profit between the big block discount and the small lot selling price. The shares may be worth buying; they may not be. Remember – there are many overvalued shares on the Stock Exchange. A proper Stock Exchange listing is no guarantee of good value.

More dubiously, some dealers will try to sell shares that are not quoted on the UK Stock Exchange. They may be shares in UK companies traded on the market made by the dealing firm. Selling such shares may not be as easy as buying them. Check back with the earlier warning about dealing in the Over-The-Counter Markets in chapter 5.

Even worse, the shares may be listed on some overseas exchange. They may be virtually unsaleable at any price. They will be pushed out by the dealers using hard-sell techniques at vastly inflated prices. Beware. Companies based in the UK, sometimes with FIMBRA membership, have tried such tricks in the past. Some have disappeared without warning, leaving investors with virtually nothing. Or they have been closed down, leaving investors to hope for some salvation from the Official Receiver many, many months later. It is growing harder for such crooks to set up here. Some may still manage it. New loopholes are always emerging.

Have no doubt. It is far better to sell your new issue through some big, boring institution you can trust than to try to cut corners dealing with someone cheaper, or more convenient. Please be warned.

Everyone should be able to find a big bank, ready to deal for them. If you want a stockbroker, watch for advertisements in the financial press. Or write to the Stock Exchange. They keep an updated list of brokers willing to take on new clients, large or small. In general, brokers outside London are better geared to dealing with small traders.

12　What it Means to be a Shareholder

If you should decide to hold on to your new issue, and join the ten million or so shareholders in the United Kingdom, a whole new world opens up before you. There is much more to being shareholder than just the chance of making a capital gain, or getting a good income on your investment. There is the fun of playing one of the most sophisticated games of all.

Investment should be fun. As you get into it, you will come to realize that almost anything can be part of the game. Share prices can be influenced by all manner of things from the weather in Siberia to the price of oil, the health of the Ayatollah, the state of the Southern Region rolling stock, the after-hours activities of Page Three models, the cost of underwear in Marks & Spencer, and so on. All human life is there somewhere behind the lists of share prices, which are moved up and down by all manner of mysterious ideas.

Reading the City pages is the ideal way to become immersed in it. The more you read, the deeper you will be lured in, the more fascinating you will find it. The money you make may become less important than playing the Stock Exchange game, and every penny up or down will matter more as a point on your personal score sheet.

WHAT YOU GET

What you actually get as a shareholder is a tiny piece of the action in the company whose shares you buy. The more shares you buy, the bigger your piece. As profits rise, so should the dividends you get on your money, and the value of your investment. The big investors who buy hundreds of thousands of pounds worth of shares may have more votes than you, but you can still stand alongside them as a shareholder, can still have a say in the affairs of your company.

Every shareholder is entitled to go to the annual meeting each year, to vote, and to ask questions. I urge every shareholder to do so. Even if you say nothing in the meeting, it gives you an ideal chance to assess the management in whom you have entrusted your money. There is nothing like meeting people face to face. Try to stay and chat to them after the meeting. Make your own judgement on whether these are the right people to run what is partly your company.

If you do decide to ask questions, it is best to submit them, in advance, in writing. You may be surprised by the trouble the chairman takes to answer you. You can stand up at the meeting and put questions. Try to make them brief, courteous and to the point. Do try to ask questions, instead of volunteering your views on the ways of the world. And do listen to the answers, and follow them up if you are not satisfied.

As a shareholder, you will already have been sent a copy of the annual report and accounts. That explains the profits in some detail, and will give a review of the past year's activities, with comments on the future. Read it carefully. It suffers from being a record of the past, when you want to know about the future. But there should be clues on the real quality of the business if you look hard enough.

The annual report will be preceded by news of the company's annual profits. Separate news of these is not usually sent to shareholders. They will be the same as those in the report and accounts. They will be covered in the press. All companies also report their half-year profits to the press. Some send printed half-year statements to shareholders at the same time as the announcement to the press. In others, it takes a while before any news is posted to shareholders.

DIVIDENDS

Most companies pay two dividends each year: an interim, or half-time, dividend plus a final dividend. The final is often the larger of the two, and shareholders will be asked to approve it at the annual meeting. The interim dividend is sent out without prior shareholder approval. The payment dates vary. Some companies send dividends soon after they are announced, or approved at the annual meeting. Others can take months. Dividends are paid after the deduction of tax at the standard rate.

PERKS

There may also be an extra bonus in the form of shareholder perks. Increasingly popular, these sometimes include a slap-up buffet lunch after the annual meeting or a bag containing samples of the company's products, given away at the annual meeting. Some companies offer cut-price samples of their products through the mail, discount vouchers to use in their shops, or even dry-cleaning at reduced rates. Cheap cross-Channel ferry tickets once made European Ferries one of the most popular shares in the country.

Being a shareholder should be an enjoyable experience. It is a way of sharing more fully in the fortunes of industry, the fortunes of the whole nation. Under the Thatcher government, it is being promoted in a much more positive light, as a way forward for everyone. That is fine. I hope it continues.

Never let that sort of thinking, and talk about the virtues of long-term investment in British industry weigh too heavily on you, especially if you are in there to make a killing in new issues. Time and again, the share speculator is portrayed as some sort of dubious character, not quite respectable, a necessary nuisance.

The new issue punter is every bit as much a part of the system as the most hide-bound City investor. You owe no allegiance to anyone in the investment world. At the core, no matter how they dress it up, it is everyone for himself – or herself. If you can have fun, and make a profit for yourself by playing the new issue game, that is all that matters. Go to it. Good luck.

Index